JAPAN'S PAST,
JAPAN'S FUTURE

Asian Voices
Series Editor: Mark Selden

Comfort Woman: A Filipina's Story of Prostitution and Slavery under the Japanese Military
by Maria Rosa Henson, introduction by Yuki Tanaka
Growing up Untouchable in India: A Dalit Autobiography
by Vasant Moon, translated by Gail Omvedt, introduction by Eleanor Zelliot
Bitter Flowers, Sweet Flowers: East Timor, Indonesia, and the World Community
edited by Richard Tanter, Mark Selden, and Stephen R. Shalom
Japan's Past, Japan's Future: One Historian's Odyssey
by Ienaga Saburō, translated and introduced by Richard H. Minear

Forthcoming Titles

Tales of Tibet: Sky Burials, Prayer Wheels, and Wind Horses
edited and translated by Herbert Batt
Voicing Concerns: Contemporary Chinese Critical Inquiry
edited by Gloria Davies, conclusion by Geremie Barmé
Rowing the Eternal Sea: The Life of a Minamata Fisherman
by Keibo Oiwa, narrated by Masato Ogata, edited by Karen Colligan-Taylor
Red Is Not the Only Color: Contemporary Chinese Fiction on Friendship, Love, and Sex between Women
edited by Patricia Sieber
Dear General MacArthur: Letters from the Japanese during the American Occupation
by Rinjiro Sodei, translated by Shizue Matsuda, edited by John Junkerman
Nineteen Years in South Korea's Gulag
by Suh Sung, translated by Jean Inglis, foreword by James Palais

JAPAN'S PAST, JAPAN'S FUTURE

One Historian's Odyssey

IENAGA SABURŌ

Translated and Introduced by Richard H. Minear

ROWMAN & LITTLEFIELD PUBLISHERS, INC.
Lanham • Boulder • New York • Oxford

ROWMAN & LITTLEFIELD PUBLISHERS, INC.

Published in the United States of America
by Rowman & Littlefield Publishers, Inc.
4720 Boston Way, Lanham, Maryland 20706
www.rowmanlittlefield.com

12 Hid's Copse Road, Cumnor Hill, Oxford OX2 9JJ, England

Cartography by Don Sluter

British Library Cataloguing in Publication Information Available

Library of Congress Cataloging-in-Publication Data
Ienaga, Saburō, 1913–
    [Ichi rekishi gakusha no ayumi. English]
    Japan's past, Japan's future : one historian's odyssey / Ienaga Saburō ;
translated and introduced by Richard H. Minear.
        p. cm.—(Asian voices)
    Includes bibliographical references and index.
    ISBN 0-7425-0988-5 (alk. paper)—ISBN 0-7425-0989-3 (pbk. : alk. paper)
        1. Ienaga, Saburō, 1913– 2. Historians—Japan—Biography. I. Minear,
Richard H. II. Title. III. Asian voices (Lanham, Md.)
    DS834.9.I35 A3   2001
    952.03'3'092—dc21
    [B]
                                                                00-062695

Printed in the United States of America

♾ ™The paper used in this publication meets the minimum requirements of
American National Standard for Information Sciences—Permanence of Paper
for Printed Library Materials, ANSI/NISO Z39.48-1992.

CONTENTS

A Note on Japanese Names and Pronunciation   *vii*

Translator's Preface   *ix*

Translator's Introduction   *1*

1   Recollections from Infancy   *27*

2   Education in the Period of Taishō Democracy and Its
    Effects on Me   *39*

3   Drawn to History: Recollections of Middle School   *49*

4   A Copernican Revolution in My Intellectual Life   *69*

5   Student Life after the Extinction of the Student
    Movement   *81*

6   My Life as a Scholar, Begun in the Era of the "Dark
    Valley"   *97*

7   My State of Mind in the Period Immediately after the
    Defeat   *123*

8   The Beginning of the Reverse Course and the
    Maturing of My Social Consciousness   *133*

9   To the Filing of the Textbook Lawsuits   *151*

10 The Textbook Trials and the Struggle at Tokyo
    University of Education   *175*

Index   *197*

About the Author and Translator   *203*

A NOTE ON JAPANESE NAMES AND PRONUNCIATION

I have kept Japanese names in Japanese order: surname first, given name second. Ienaga is the historian's family name; Saburō, his given name.

Japanese names and words are not difficult to pronounce. There is little stress on one syllable over others; vowel sounds are close to those of Spanish or Italian; long marks simply prolong the same sound. Ienaga is a four-syllable name, with all four syllables getting equal stress: Ee [as in the letter E], eh [as in the initial sound of the verb excite], na [as in *not*], wa [as in *wa*ll]. His given name is Sa [as in *sa*lt], bu [as in *boo*m], rō [two-syllables, the sound of *ro*tation, slightly prolonged].

TRANSLATOR'S PREFACE

Thirty-five years ago, I was a Fulbright graduate student at Kyoto University, studying Japanese constitutional theories of the late nineteenth century; that research became my first book, *Japanese Tradition and Western Law*. Ienaga Saburō had written on the topic in the previous decade. In my research I discovered materials—early writings of an important conservative scholar—that Ienaga had not known about. Disregarding the vast difference in age and stature between us, I sent Ienaga a copy of an essay introducing these materials, and he responded with a kind note. In 1967, in *Studies in the Modern Constitutional Ideas of Japan* (p. 77, n. 8), he noted my contribution.

At the University of Massachusetts, I came up for tenure in the early 1970s. When the history department asked for a list of scholars familiar with my work, I included Ienaga. The department sent him my résumé, which by then included *Victors' Justice: The Tokyo War Crimes Trial* (1971; Japanese translation, 1972; to be reissued in 2001 by the Center for Japanese Studies, University of Michigan). In that book, writing under the heavy impact of my own opposition to the American war in Vietnam, I attacked the Tokyo Trial from many angles. Soon Ienaga published an essay in the journal *Misuzu* attacking my interpretation of the Tokyo Trial, an interpretation he learned of in evaluating my work. I responded in the same journal. The narrow issue we debated in print was how to read the dissenting opinion of the Indian judge, Radhabinod Pal. Ienaga saw in Pal's convoluted prose an anti-Communism willing to excuse the excesses of Japan's wartime leaders, who were staunch anti-Communists; I saw in it a search for alternatives to the Allied propaganda claims and judicial charges of blatant Japanese aggression. Ienaga's reading of Pal's

ix

dissent was of a piece with his larger intellectual agenda, including his intense aversion to the fifteen-year war and his fear of the resurgence in postwar Japan of the antidemocratic forces he blames for the war. My reading was of a piece with my own more modest goal of alerting American readers to American myopia and prejudice about Japan and of attacking American imperialism. (I have never seen Ienaga's letter evaluating my work, but I assume that he wrote one; I did get tenure. In retrospect, I am appalled by the imposition on his time, for by then—as I know now—he was utterly consumed in the two fights that form the focus of chapters 9 and 10 of this autobiography.)

In 1983 he and I met for the first time, in Tokyo at a conference on the Tokyo Trial. On the second and final day, he and I shared the platform. Our papers and the discussion that followed are available in English in *The Tokyo Trial: An International Symposium*. *The Works of Ienaga Saburō* includes Ienaga's attack on my work in one volume and quotes from my statement at the conference in another; I am honored to be included. I still think Ienaga was mistaken about Justice Pal. But my respect for Ienaga is enormous. And in the course of translating this autobiography, that respect has grown. In the second half of his life Ienaga has encountered many of the issues that historians of conscience in the United States and other industrialized societies face today: how to resist the master narrative of the state, battle censorship and the conservative push for national standards and achievement testing to enforce those standards, and fight off restrictions on the academic freedoms that many in the academy—at least in the United States—have taken for granted.

For help in preparing this volume, I wish to thank first and foremost Yasuko Fukumi, who helped me as she helped me with earlier translation projects. Second, Ienaga Saburō himself, for setting an example from which we can all learn and, of course, for permission to translate and for supplying copies of many of the photographs. Thanks as well go to Mark Selden of the State University of New York at Binghamton, Susan McEachern of Rowman & Littlefield, Inokuchi Hiromichi and Nozaki Yoshiko, Laura Hein, and Don Sluter.

JAPAN'S PAST,
JAPAN'S FUTURE

Ienaga Saburō addresses supporters, February 1994. Photo courtesy of the National League for Support of the School Textbook Screening Suit.

TRANSLATOR'S INTRODUCTION

Ienaga Saburō is Japan's single most famous historian. He is famous among Japanese historians; he is famous as well among the public. His prime field of concern is Japanese intellectual history, and he has transformed that field in important ways. But he is famous today primarily for his role in two political actions: his lawsuits against the Ministry of Education, to stop its attempts to alter the textbooks he wrote for use in Japan's schools, and his battle against moving his university's campus from Tokyo to the new "Tsukuba Research City." Ask the stereotypical Japanese person on the street to name a historian, and chances are good you will hear Ienaga's name.

As one of Japan's foremost intellectuals, Ienaga is by definition a world-class intellectual, even if the world outside Japan has paid him little attention. Several of his major works are available in translation: two in English and German; one each in French, Spanish, and Russian. But Ienaga suffers the parochial neglect with which the English-speaking world (particularly the American world) treats thinkers from outside Europe and the United States. Ask even a well-educated American to name non-English-language intellectual giants of the twentieth century, and one hears the names of Sartre, Camus, Foucault, or Habermas. But a Japanese (or Indian, Chinese, or Vietnamese) name? Unlikely. It is not that thinkers from these cultures are less significant than their European counterparts; it is that most of us don't know of them. We cannot read their works (there are very few translations in the social sciences—novels, yes; monographs, no), so we don't review them or cite them. Knowing little about the contexts in which they operate, we don't appreciate their contributions or see their potential as role models for us. With this translation I hope

1

to help remedy this ignorance in the case of Ienaga and to demonstrate that Ienaga's work is of significance beyond Japan, indeed, to all who study history and to all who honor the fight against government intrusion into education and the realm of the mind.

Ienaga Saburō (Ienaga is the family name; here and throughout I leave Japanese names in their Japanese order) was born in September 1913 in Nagoya. Today he lives in retirement in suburban Tokyo. He is an improbable octogenarian, for he was sickly as a child, unfit physically—to his great relief—for military service, and condemned, by the chronic indigestion that has been his lot, to live an ascetic life. That life spans Japan's twentieth century, one of the most dramatic and traumatic periods in Japan's history and perhaps in the history of the world.

Speaking in 1986 to a friendly audience, Ienaga noted the changes he has witnessed in his long life:

> Weak in body and with no prospect of long life, I lived my youth during the fifteen-year war [Ienaga's preferred term for Japan's wars of 1931–1945] that cost untold millions of war dead. I can't help thinking it miraculous that today I am still alive at seventy-two, even as I am all too conscious that my powers of mind and body decline with each year. Yet the seven decades I have lived represent an age of convulsion upon convulsion, a succession of great and radical social and cultural change unprecedented in Japanese history.[1]

It is an era, he suggests, far fuller even than the era of Japan's late nineteenth century, when some people born in the Edo era lived to see Imperial Japan's success in the Russo-Japanese War of 1904–1905.

Ienaga started academic life as a student of the intellectual history of seventh-century Japanese Buddhism. Although this era is of enormous importance in Japanese history, linguistic difficulties and distance in time from the present make its study a bookish pursuit. Its practitioners live in a rarefied atmosphere. But Ienaga's experience in the war and his involvement with textbooks and activism brought him down to earth, so it is not sur-

---

1. Ienaga Saburō, *"Gekidō shichijūnen no rekishi o ikite"* (December 1986), *Hyōgen: Tōkyō kyōiku daigaku Nihonshi kenkyūkai—sotsugyō jūshūnen kinen;* in *Ienaga Saburō shū* (16 vols.; Iwanami, 1997–1999), 16:258.

prising that in tracing the changes though which he has lived, he focuses on daily life:

> Even looking at the most practical side of things, when I was a child, children in the countryside wore only Japanese clothes. [Ienaga doesn't need to tell his Japanese audience that by 1986 Japanese children all wore T-shirts, most if not all manufactured in China or the United States.] In Tokyo some children wore Western clothes, but more than half went to school in Japanese clothes. Virtually no adult females wore Western clothes. Homes were all tatami-style, and only the "bourgeois" could afford to live in houses with one Western room furnished with tables and chairs; in the houses of common people there were no telephones and of course no cars. Only heads of firms or high officials at the ministerial level had cars for private use. Before radio, the mass entertainment that drew the largest crowds was "moving pictures," but these were silent films that came with a live commentator/narrator and brass band, and of course they were black-and-white. In the winters one barely got through with coal-burning hibachis and in the summers, with hand fans or at most an electric fan. Horse-drawn carts and ox carts carrying human feces made their way through downtown Tokyo.[2]

But by the end of his life Japan was among the most modern of modern states, in few material ways significantly different from the United States or Western Europe. In Japan the transformation did come more quickly, leaving those like Ienaga, who remember the 1910s and 1920s, even more bemused than Americans of similar age.

Ienaga's academic career stretched from his first appointment as researcher in Tokyo (1937, when Ienaga was twenty-four), to a stint at Niigata Higher School (1941–1943), to Tokyo Higher Normal School and its successor university, Tokyo University of Education (1944–1977). He lectured or offered courses at many other universities. Ienaga's major scholarly works in the years between 1941 and 1967 include the following: *The Logic of Negation in the Intellectual History of Japan* (1941), *Theories of Kingship of Shōtoku Taishi* (1942), *Chronology of Early Paintings in the Ya-*

---

2. *Ienaga Saburō shū,* pp. 258–259.

mato Style (1942), *Studies in Early Buddhist Intellectual History* (1942), *The Development of a Religious View of Nature in Japanese Intellectual History* (1944), *History of Early Painting in the Yamato Style* (1946), *Studies in Medieval Buddhist Intellectual History* (1947), *On the Assimilation of Foreign Culture* (1948), *The Modern Spirit and Its Limitations* (1950), *Studies in the Modern Intellectual History of Japan* (1953), *History of Japanese Ethical Thought* (1954), *The Life of a Singular Thinker: Taoka Reiun—Man and Ideas* (1955), *Precursor of Revolutionary Ideas: Ueki Emori—Man and Ideas* (1955), *Ueki Emori Studies* (1960), *Struggle against Governmental Wrong: The Life and Thought of Masaki Hiroshi* (1964), *An Intellectual Historical Study of Minobe Tatsukichi* (1964), and *Studies in Modern Japanese Constitutional Ideas* (1967). As these titles indicate, Ienaga began with Buddhist intellectual history and art history of the period before A.D. 1000 but moved on, in the years after the war, to nineteenth- and twentieth-century social and intellectual history. Indeed, he moved on to figures—Uchimura, Ueki, Taoka, Masaki, Minobe—who spoke out or struggled against the status quo.

The years after the war also saw a stream of books that arose from Ienaga's entanglements with the Japanese state. These books include *History and Education* (1956), *History and the Present* (1959), *Criticism of the Courts* (1959), *A Historical Analysis of Judicial Independence* (1962), *A History of the Independence of the University* (1962), *Textbook Certification* (1965), and *A Historian's View of Constitutional and Educational Issues* (1965). The 1999 bibliography of his writings runs to over one hundred pages and, to mention only book-length monographs (not edited works, annotated editions, textbooks, reprints, or updated versions), seven before 1945 and forty-odd between 1947 and 1971. The *Works of Ienaga Saburō* (sixteen volumes), published in 1997–1999, includes quite literally only a fraction of his books, essays, and reviews.

Those who cannot read Japanese can approach Ienaga's historical scholarship in several ways. In 1965 the American sociologist Robert N. Bellah, then in his late thirties, produced a survey of Ienaga's writings in intellectual history through the early 1960s. "Ienaga Saburō and the Search for Meaning in Modern Japan" is a highly sympathetic treatment that traces Ienaga's grappling with "what are clearly existential questions for him" and focuses on Ienaga's encounters (in *The Logic of Negation*, published in 1941) with the Buddhist thinkers Shōtoku Taishi and

Shinran. Bellah finds Ienaga "always historical rather than abstract" in reaching "a denial of every element in the tradition which was not itself premised on denial"—a position remarkable, to say the least, in the hypercharged ultranationalist days of the fifteen-year war. Bellah notes the trend in Ienaga's thought after 1940 to confront Japan's nineteenth- and twentieth-century intellectual history and "social responsibility" and to see the Christian Uchimura Kanzō as the most "modern" of Japan's modern thinkers. Bellah notes "a correspondence between [Ienaga's] own experience and the 'logic of negation' of Shōtoku Taishi and Shinran" but misses one implication of that most important of Ienaga's wartime books: that Japan's modern counterpart to Shōtoku and Shinran may soon emerge. It is almost as if Ienaga sees himself in that role, the person who embodies in his life and work the next major step forward in Japanese culture. As we shall see, ambition is not foreign to Ienaga's makeup. But Bellah is absolutely correct in seeing that Ienaga has searched "the whole course of Japanese history" and developed a "general schema." This scheme stands in sharp contrast both to the ultranationalist veneration of a largely mythical Japanese tradition and to the Marxist reduction of ideas to epiphenomena of the superstructure. Bellah argues that under the impetus of his own intellectual/spiritual odyssey, Ienaga has recast Japanese intellectual history.[3]

A second route to Ienaga is through translations of his works. In 1953 the Tourist Library published a truncated version of one of his textbooks: *History of Japan*. In 1973 another Japanese publisher

---

3. Robert N. Bellah, "Ienaga Saburō and the Search for Meaning in Modern Japan," in Marius B. Jansen, ed., *Changing Japanese Attitudes toward Modernization* (Princeton, 1965), pp. 369–423. Other reports in English include John Caiger, "Ienaga Saburō and the First Postwar Japanese History Textbook," *Modern Asian Studies* 3, no. 1 (1969): 1–17; R. P. Dore, "Notes and Comment: Textbook Censorship in Japan: The Ienaga Case," *Pacific Affairs* 43, no. 4 (Winter 1970–1971): 548–556; Benjamin Duke, "The Textbook Controversy," *Japan Quarterly* 19, no. 3 (July–September 1972): 337–352. More recent accounts include: Nozaki Yoshiko and Inokuchi Hiromitsu, "Japanese Education, Nationalism, and Ienaga Saburō's Textbook Lawsuits," in Laura Hein and Mark Selden, eds., *Censoring History: Perspectives on Nationalism and War in the Twentieth Century* (M. E. Sharpe, 2000), pp. 96–126, and Nozaki Yoshiko, "Textbook Controversy and the Production of Public Truth: Japanese Education, Nationalism, and Saburo Ienaga's Court Challenges," (Ph.D. diss., University of Wisconsin, 2000). See also Takashi Yoshida, "A Battle over History: The Nanjing Massacre in Japan," in Joshua A. Fogel, ed., *The Nanjing Massacre in History and Historiography* (University of California, 2000), pp. 70–132.

brought out his survey *Painting in the Yamato Style* (trans. John M. Shields). In 1978 Pantheon Press published *The Pacific War, 1931–1945* (trans. Frank Baldwin; there is also a Spanish translation of 1982). In 1990 a German press published *Kulturgeschichte Japans,* a translation by Karl Friedrich Zahn of the second edition (1983) of *Nihon bunkashi.* In preparation is a French translation: *Logique de Négation: le développement d'une logique de négation dans histoire de la pensée Japonaise.*

The most accessible of these (it is still in print today) is *The Pacific War, 1931–1945: A Critical Perspective on Japan's Role in World War II,* a book of 1968, the year after he published the first edition of this autobiography. Ienaga intended, he writes in the preface to the English edition, that this book would "show the Japanese people the naked realities of the Pacific War. My objective was to stimulate reflection and self-criticism about the war." Ienaga traces this objective to his own experience. In testimony before one of the courts that heard his suits, Ienaga expressed it this way:

> I repeat that I am a member of the prewar generation, and on account of that reckless war several million of my generation died cruel deaths either in the wastes of the continent, in the ocean depths, or deep in the jungle. They died cruel deaths in the air raids, in the atomic bombings. I was fortunate and survived. However, I had been guilty of being unable to do anything for my homeland to stop this senseless war and of simply looking on as my homeland went to its destruction, and I found that truly inexcusable. To be told to write nice things about the war again, to whip Japan up once again to war, this time in subjection to the United States—I had to resist such education policies; otherwise, on my deathbed I would relive the remorse I felt then: once again, back then, why didn't I act? I don't want to relive that remorse. I'm one citizen with little power, but I wanted to atone, if only one part in ten thousand, for the sin of not having opposed the war, and it was that frame of mind that emboldened me to lodge these suits.[4]

---

4. Statement under direct examination, Tokyo District Court, Civil Bench 2 (Judge Sugimoto presiding), July 12, 1969; in Ienaga Saburō, *Ienaga Saburō kyōiku saiban shōgenshū* (Hitotsubashi shobō, 1972), p. 158. (Hereafter *Shōgenshū.*)

American readers in particular need to exercise care in reading Ienaga's book on the war. Ienaga blames Japan for the war, and lazy readers may conclude, "Aha! The United States *was* right." Ienaga's attack on Japan's policies and actions seems to confirm the American master narrative of the Pacific War. But that is a superficial reading that ignores the context in which, and the audience for whom, Ienaga wrote: not Americans, but Japanese. I have experienced something similar myself. Japanese reactionaries have taken my own *Victors' Justice: The Tokyo War Crimes Trial,* available since 1972 in Japanese translation, as evidence to support their view of the war: if the trial was a travesty, then perhaps Japan's wartime leaders were not criminal. For the same reason Japanese such as Ienaga on the left have viewed the book with grave suspicion. Translations make it possible for those of us who do not read a given language to make contact with the culture that supports it; they do not solve the problems of comprehension and evaluation. The underlying issues in this case—the root causes of the Pacific War, the roles of Japanese and American (and British, Russian, German, and Chinese) policy in leading to war, the war's role in world history—are very real and still the subject of significant scholarly debate.

In his preface, Ienaga writes:

> I decided at the outset not to treat certain problems beyond my competence: the economic causes of the war, the machinations of the ruling elite, diplomatic negotiations, the details of battles and campaigns, and the war policies of other countries. Instead, I brought my special training to bear upon a few basic issues, trusting that if I stressed these major matters, the most important questions about the war would not be slighted. . . . I wanted . . . to reach the core of the war and its lessons for the Japanese people.

What is that core? The key lies in part 1: "Why Was the War Not Prevented?" Of the three chapters that form part 1, one deals with Japanese racism toward their neighbors, notably China and Korea; one, with thought control and indoctrination (by 1968 Ienaga had already lodged two of his suits against the Ministry of Education); and one, with the authoritarian and irrational military, of which—we learn in this autobiography—Ienaga's own father had once been an officer. In short, Japan's *domestic* history—political and cultural—explains the war. Had Japan been less racist and more democratic and had its military been less irrational, the war would not have happened. Ienaga has high praise for the 8th Route Army of China's Communists under Mao Zedong, which leads hasty readers to conclude that Ienaga has Marxist sympathies; but what appeals to him about the Chinese Communists is precisely their *democracy*. (Similarly, Ienaga reacted to the fall of the Soviet Union in an interview of 1992: "I think the key to the Soviet Union's collapse lies in the fact that the one-party dictatorship of the Communist Party suppressed freedom."[5]) To this translator, who has studied the Pacific War and found much to criticize in *American* policy and diplomacy, Ienaga's analysis is at best one part of a very complicated story. A history of World War II without economics, diplomatic negotiations, the war policies of other countries? Unlikely. But Ienaga's major concern is with *Japanese* issues, with Japanese racist attitudes toward and mistreatment of its Asian neighbors, and with keeping alive in Japan a strong awareness of "the horrors of war" (a chapter title), not with American or geopolitical concerns. And central to those domestic issues is the one that has made Ienaga a household name in Japan: education. In testimony in his court suits Ienaga focused on this connection:

> I don't know because I'm not a specialist on the West, so this is no more than hearsay knowledge; but in the West the point of departure of "public education" was home schooling by parents, and the state took over the burden of education from the parents gradually—that's how public education developed. But in Japan that wasn't the case: in the Tokugawa period parents sent their children to temple schools or academies, and in that sense "private" education was very well developed; however, modern education after 1868 didn't develop on that basis but under great political demands imposed by the rapid development of capitalism, it was propelled from the top down, quickly and in some sense at great strain. In the process . . . those running the state pulled people along in the

---

5. Interview with Osanai Mieko (January 20, 1992), in Ienaga Saburō, *Ienaga Saburō taidanshū: Kyōkasho no 30-nen* (Minshūsha, 1995), pp. 130–131. (Hereafter *Taidanshū*.)

direction the leaders wanted to go. . . . In some sense improvement in the people's educational level took place at the sacrifice of the people's freedom and their manifold potential.

The tragedy of Japan that led to the Pacific War is a result of various political, social, and economic causes, but one important cause lies here: that the vast majority of the people were educated from youth into a frame of mind in which they could not criticize state policies independently but had to follow along in those policies, mistaken though they were. Education since 1868 carries heavy responsibility for bringing on that tragedy. Moreover, via the sudden plunge into the Pacific War[,] education itself was fundamentally destroyed.[6]

Education and the war; the war and education: here are the fundamental focuses of Ienaga's public career.

Ienaga is a household word in Japan today because of his activism, because he took a leading role in two long-running disputes. One dispute involved the fight against governmental control of educational content; it took the form of his three lawsuits (1965–1997) against the Ministry of Education (see chapter 9). In Japan as in many European countries, the national Ministry of Education plays a much more important role than does the Department of Education in the United States. For example, in Japan, the Ministry "certifies" textbooks, and only textbooks so "certified" can be used in Japan's schools. (In prewar days the Ministry *compiled* the textbooks.) Hence bureaucrats make judgments on balance, tone, and coverage. And in the years in which Ienaga did battle with them, these bureaucrats had either personal roots in the prewar era or close ties to conservative politicians.

For virtually the entire postwar era the Japanese political system has been firmly in the control of the Liberal-Democratic Party, which is neither liberal nor democratic. One prime minister, Kishi Nobusuke (in office 1957–1960), had been a Class A war crimes suspect; he escaped inclusion in the dock at the Tokyo Trial only by the luck of the draw. A second prime minister, Satō Eisaku (in office 1964–1972), was Kishi's younger brother (Kishi had been adopted out of his birth family). Like the Supreme Court

---

6. Statement under direct examination in suit of Osaka teachers' union (May 28, 1963); in *Shōgenshū*, pp. 55–56.

Figure I.1   March 16, 1993, Japan's major newspapers react to the Supreme Court's rejection of Ienaga's appeal in the first lawsuit with front-page coverage. In the front is the Asahi's *evening edition, the headline across the top (left to right) reads, "Mr. Ienaga's Appeal Turned Back: Confirmation of the Rejection of a 28-Year Struggle." The vertical headline along the right side reads, "Judgment Affirms Constitutionality of Certification." The photo is of Ienaga, and he is quoted as reacting with outrage to the Supreme Court's "contemptuous" dismissal of his appeal.*

In the middle is the Yomiuri's *evening edition, with horizontal headline, "First Supreme Court Verdict: Textbook Certification Constitutional." At the back is the* Mainichi's *evening edition, with the horizontal headline, "Supreme Court: 'Textook Certification Constitutional.'" The photograph in the oval is of Ienaga.*

in the United States, the Ministry of Education in Japan follows the ballot box, and the periods in which it has pushed its conservative agenda most aggressively are those periods of particular Liberal-Democratic electoral success. A conservative electoral sweep in June 1980 led to the most recent chapter in the textbook saga.[7] In the United States in 1994 the Republican landslide in the off-year elections led to the fiasco at the Smithsonian Institution, when congressional and other pressures forced the gutting of an exhibit on the *Enola Gay,* the plane that dropped the atomic bomb on Hiroshima, and the purge of the Smithsonian's executives. American intellectuals experienced then the threat that Japanese intellectuals like Ienaga have lived with for decades—that politicians and their bureaucratic allies impose on the nation's cultural institutions a party line that flies in the face of scholarly consensus. The debacle at the Smithsonian may give Americans a new appreciation for the context in which Ienaga has operated since the late 1940s.

The second major issue on which Ienaga fought was the plan to move Tokyo University of Education out of the capital city and to the then-new "Tsukuba Science City" about an hour east of Tokyo to become Tsukuba University. This controversy began in the late 1960s and ended with the move in the early 1970s; Ienaga's retirement from teaching coincided with the death of Tokyo University of Education. As Ienaga describes it here (chapter 10), the move gutted the university with the most democratic governance in Japan and created in its place a research university run in autocratic fashion, from the top down. Ienaga was among the leaders of the doomed fight against the move, and his role led the opposition to call for his head. In Ienaga's mind these two struggles were interconnected: not only were democratic principles at stake in both fights, but also numerous individuals lined up on the same side of each. Ienaga had little hope of prevailing on either issue, and he realized that fact; but for him the struggle itself held profound significance, both for him personally—he had not opposed the Pacific War—and for Japan.

These two struggles came at the height of Ienaga's career.

---

7. Cf. Chong-sik Lee, "History and Politics in Japanese-Korean Relations: The Textbook Controversy and Beyond," *Journal of Northeast Asian Studies* 2, no. 4 (December 1983): 69–93.

Photo I.1 October 20, 1993, Ienaga Saburō (holding banner and wearing hat) and supporters march in protest against the Tokyo Higher Court's ruling in the third lawsuit. The banner reads: "10.20 [October 20] Tokyo Higher Court Decision: Don't Accept Textbook Certification That Fosters a Warped View of Invasion." (Photo courtesy of National League for Support of the School Textbook Screening Suit, whose name in Japanese forms the bottom line of the banner.)

They began when he was in his mid-fifties. Ienaga himself comments caustically, this time in 1978:

> I spent my youth under the oppressive regime based on the Peace Preservation Laws [1925] and in the fires of war, and I had no opportunity to experience the *Sturm und Drang* appropriate to youth, so how ironic to have that experience at Tokyo University of Education only in my declining years! Unable after the barricades went up to get to my office or the department, using the facilities of the attached high school late into the night to plan out next steps, facing harsh kangaroo court at the hands of students, and in particular the Humanities Faculty's being driven into a tight corner in the era of despotic rule after Dean Miyajima brought in the riot squad and experiencing repeated clashes over policy differences even with colleagues who like me opposed the move to Tsukuba—those hardships are beyond my power to describe.[8]

An unlikely activist, Ienaga proved a surprisingly effective one. Here is his final statement as litigant in the third of the three lawsuits; the date is October 26, 1992:

> Today, twenty-eight years after I lodged the first suit . . . I should like to state one wish. Having lived thirty-two years under the Meiji Constitution, I can only have sad thoughts when I recall how great was the damage it caused: on the formulation of knowledge, information, and ideas under state control of the educational content. . . .
>   Under the Constitution of Japan [1946], too, despite the fact that it guarantees freedom of thought as a fundamental human right, the state's control of knowledge, information, and ideas has not disappeared, and it is indeed a cause for heartfelt regret that we see the state's intrusion into various fields. . . . [I]n textbook certification that interference appears in crudest form and throws a dark shadow on the . . . nation for the next generation.
>   . . . I have had to carry on such lengthy suits for one reason, and only one: that court judgments applying the brakes to the tightening of textbook certification have not been issued.

---

8. Ienaga Saburō, *Tōkyō kyōiku daigaku bungakubu: Eikō to junan no sanjūnen* (Tokuma, 1978), p. 241.

The Supreme Court's judgment on textbook certification has not yet been handed down, but I hope Supreme Court judgments are issued on the basis of lower court judgments that are based on examination of the facts and are well-matched with the ideals of the Constitution. . . .

Gentlemen of the Court: I hope that you render a fine decision worthy of becoming the foundation of legal progress in an even better direction and of showing not simply to Japan but also to the peoples of the world the true prestige of the Japanese judiciary.

But Ienaga was speaking to justices for whom a finding against the government would have been extraordinary, and they rejected most of his contentions.[9]

Ienaga's efforts found greater resonance and appreciation among his professional colleagues and among the general public. The Ienaga lawsuits form a chapter in postwar Japan's politics of protest, a chapter that has yet to be written. The cause involved thousands of people, from all over Japan, who contributed their time and energy and money so that the lawsuits could go forward. Almost as important for our purposes, and far easier to document, is the impact of the suits on Japan's historians. The ranks of those historians who took part—conducting research, discussing strategies, testifying in court, organizing support—include many prominent historians in Ienaga's generation and in those generations that have followed his. Here is one assessment by a contemporary, who wrote in 1981:

The support movement behind Ienaga's lawsuits is both a struggle aimed at abolishing the system of textbook certification and an effort to make historical studies themselves deeper and more creative. . . . Up till now we have barely touched upon fundamental examination of the important issues of how to organize and narrate survey histories. And in rebutting the improper demands of the textbook certifiers, we

9. Cf. Lawrence W. Beer, "Japan's Constitutional System and Its Judicial Interpretation," in John O. Haley, ed., *Law and Society in Contemporary Japan: American Perspectives* (Kendall/Hunt, 1988), pp. 7–35, esp. p. 15: "Since 1947, the judges of Japan have cautiously built a new, more visible, more independent, and more powerful judicial institution . . . but the Supreme Court has chosen a markedly deferential role toward the Diet and administrators when dealing with some constitutional issues."

have exposed issues and areas where research has been inade-
quate, and we have gone to work with the tools of positivistic
research. Concrete examples are women's history and the history of manners and customs. The ordering of the history of
historiography: that, too, is one harvest the support movement has produced, but we have only just begun, and the ordering isn't yet settled on and remains as a task for the future.

We can only be grateful that the textbook suits have provided us with new research topics, one after the other, and
that we have had the opportunity to do group research toward
their solution.[10]

And here a younger historian, speaking in 1998:

At the time [the late 1970s] what we felt was that if we took
part, we would strengthen our problem-consciousness, but we
were acutely aware of the difficulty of merging problem-
consciousness and research: how after all to bring that and
our own research together?

But because we had the terrific example of Ienaga, even
if we suffered, we had to carry on. [Laughter.] I think this is
the problem that many face in taking part in a scholars' movement; but more important than the suffering is how to over-
come this problem, how to extricate oneself from it.[11]

Here three historians elaborate on those remarks. They are all at
least thirty-two years younger than Ienaga (they were born in
1947, 1956, and 1945, respectively), and they had all taken part
in the support movement. Their remarks came in a symposium in
1998:

Yasuda Hiroshi: I too was on the movement staff at the time,
took part in working groups, and compensated participants;
but I have the strong impression that our work involved the
very best fit between the social significance or social responsibility of history and its scholarly content. Speaking for myself,
taking part in the discussions [in the working groups], I

10. Tōyama Shigeki, *Kyōkasho kentei no shisō to rekishi kyōiku: rekishi gakusha wa shōgensuru* (Ayumi shuppan, 1983), pp. 6–7.
11. Emura Eiichi, in *"Zadankai: Kyōkasho saiban shien undō no sanjūninen,"* in *Rekishi no hōtei: Ienaga kyōkasho saiban to rekishigaku* (Ōtsuki, 1998), p. 190. (Here-after *Rekishi no hōtei.*)

learned an awful lot of history. In classes in my university days I heard virtually nothing about historical method. But in coming to grips with real life, and in the form of the points at issue in court, we studied in depth how to think about the scholarly methods of history and the problem of the social function of history, the two issues collapsed into one. I have the strong impression that in that sense it was enormously helpful in forming my own view of history.

Moritani Kimitoshi: The same holds true for me. . . . I was twenty-five then [1981] and a specialist on ancient Greece, right in the middle of writing my thesis. At first, no one knew who I was, and I was mistaken for a right-winger. [Chuckle.] But in my student days I too hadn't studied history itself in any serious way, so listening to the discussion, I thought to myself, "Yes, this is what the discipline of history is all about," and for the first time I understood. That courtroom was a university.

Kimijima Kazuhiko: Afterwards all kinds of related essays appeared in journals like *Rekishigaku kenkyū*, *Rekishi hyōron,* and *Nihonshi kenkyū*. Taking off from the discussions within the working groups, the authors had deepened their own studies. And among those who published books at this time, many noted in preface or afterword that they had participated in the lawsuits. In that sense there were a lot of folks, I think, who weren't merely assisting with support of the lawsuits but in the process learned and saw the effects on their own scholarship.[12]

In both wars—in court and at Tokyo University of Education—Ienaga lost all but a few battles. Still, history's verdict on the wars is not yet in. For thirty years Ienaga issued a serious challenge to the authority of the state in matters of the mind and to comfortable interpretations of the war and Japanese colonialism. Had Ienaga not existed, the left would have been forced to invent him.

Ienaga's fame today is in large part the result of his activism, but his legacy will be as much intellectual as activist. Indeed, Ienaga's life and work have great internal consistency. Ienaga ends his autobiography (first edition) in 1967 and (second edition) in 1975—nearly a quarter of a century ago. This fact leaves us wish-

---

12. *Rekishi no hōtei*, pp. 203–204.

ing for something more up to date, more contemporary. But perhaps we underestimate the basic continuity: who Ienaga was in 1965 and who he became by 1999 are different only in degree of media attention. In 1965 Ienaga was a relatively obscure historian; at the end of his life Ienaga is the single most famous historian of his time. But the Ienaga of the last twenty-five years, since he has published the second edition of this autobiography, is the Ienaga of the first sixty years. One of the most insightful essays on Ienaga's ideas dates to 1965, over thirty-five years ago and just about the time Ienaga completed his autobiography (first edition). The author is Kuroha Kiyotaka (1934–1987), colleague of Ienaga and specialist in education. Ienaga himself thought so much of the essay—it "explained me to myself"[13]—that he had it republished in the first issue of the monthly that accompanied the publication of his sixteen-volume selected works. I offer this summation here for the same reason.

Prominent in Kuroha's analysis is Ienaga's "initial intent" (*shoshin*). *Shoshin* is a difficult word to translate. The *sho* of *shoshin* means "first, original"; the *shin* means "heart" or "mind" or "soul." The term goes back to ancient Japanese; it has Buddhist overtones. The great Noh playwright Zeami (fourteenth century) spoke of "not losing one's *shoshin*." *Shoshin* in this usage is thought to mean the arts one learned on first becoming a Noh actor and one's freshness at that time, one's humility, and one's high tension and moral resolve. These ethical overtones make Kuroha's choice of words particularly effective to describe Ienaga. There is no exact English equivalent. Perhaps we point to the same sense when we speak of "selling out" or "getting co-opted." What is it we lose when we sell out? Our early idealism, dedication, freshness, purity, humility. These are a large part of the Japanese term.

Let us follow Kuroha's argument. Kuroha begins by looking for the genesis of the lawsuits in Ienaga's scholarship and character. He writes: "The human characteristic that runs through the two suits is fierce expectation of the Constitution of Japan [1946], which had been achieved at the sacrifice of innumerable lives." And this characteristic permeates Ienaga's history-writing: "In

---

13. Ienaga, *Ienaga Saburō shū Geppō #1* (November 1997), p. 1. (Hereafter *Geppō.*)

the very structure of Ienaga's history-writing, the germ of the Ienaga suits has long been nourished." The suits, coming late in Ienaga's life, yet represent "the meeting point of the scholarly struggle and the popular struggle."

Kuroha is bold to insist that there is a unifying thread in Ienaga's history-writing, for Ienaga has tackled one topic after another, one century after another, one thinker after another. Indeed, Kuroha sees this "ceaseless movement of research topic . . . that knows neither pause nor stagnation" as a defining characteristic of Ienaga's scholarship. But Kuroha suggests that Ienaga's "ambitious plan to establish the genealogy of uncertainty about the value of human life . . . springs from the strong self-awareness about the limits of human life of the sickly Ienaga." Ienaga's history-writing "draws on the deepest wellsprings of Ienaga Saburō's *kokoro.*" This term *kokoro*—"heart, soul, mind"—is a different reading of the character that is the *shin* of *shoshin.* Zeami admonished his disciples not to forget their *shoshin;* Ienaga, writes Kuroha, "*cannot* forget his *shoshin.*"

Ienaga combines in his character absolutely contradictory elements: abstinence and passion, personal ambition and devotion to the most textually precise scholarship. To Kuroha, these characteristics are all interrelated. The "depth of the ethic of abstinence parallels the strength of passion that consumes" Ienaga. His abstinence—in significant measure imposed on him by his poor health—is the reverse side of his passion. His absolute commitment to careful textual scholarship (Kuroha calls it "positivism") is the reverse side of his absolute ambition. Kuroha continues: "To proceed by objectivizing positivistically as much as possible his own humanity . . . is the way, for Ienaga's history-writing, to deal with Ienaga Saburō the person." Ienaga's history-writing is "a scholarship of subjectivity," "a scholarship of confession." Ienaga's *shoshin* is a centripetal force; his positivism is a centrifugal force. The two balance each other: "If that were not the case, who on earth could stand up to the stress of . . . drowning in the sea of evidence in order to give true life to one's *shoshin?*" In other words, the moral drive of the *shoshin* and the inductive force of the positivism stand in direct opposition. Here is Ienaga in the preface to his intellectual-historical study of Minobe Tatsukichi (1963), the towering figure of liberal constitutional theory of the first half of the twentieth century, the author of the theory that the emperor is an organ of the state, a man with whom Ienaga had personal contact during the war (see chapter 6): "At least for myself, intellectual history would have held little attraction" if one could not connect it with the present. Ienaga writes: "For us living in the present, what meaning does Minobe's thinking hold?" There lies Ienaga's true interest. Ienaga's history-writing is at the same time autobiography; it is "apology."

Ienaga, Kuroha writes, has focused on figures who were strong characters, confident in their subjectivity (*shutaisei*). Like *shoshin, shutaisei* is difficult to translate exactly; one of Japan's major intellectual debates in the 1950s concerned *shutaisei.* Many proponents felt *shutaisei* was a core value of "modernity," yet they found it sadly lacking in Japan. Kuroha writes: "His choice of topics has a virtually automatic tendency to weigh the strength of *shutaisei.*" The strong egos of the individuals Ienaga has chosen to focus his research on lead in Ienaga's mind to a "thorough and principled democracy/republicanism" that refuses to countenance "turning people into *means.*" Kuroha cites Kant's imperative— "act so as to treat every man as an end, never merely as a means." It is this formulation, Kuroha writes, that leads to the Ienaga lawsuits.

The lawsuits are a product, Kuroha suggests, of Ienaga's "re-recognition of democracy as a trans-class, trans-era value." After all, Ienaga had praised legal scholar Minobe Tatsukichi's "spirit of resistance to the abuse of government power." And for Ienaga, Kuroha writes, the lawsuits represent that same spirit of resistance: "The principles of democracy crystallized in the Constitution of Japan were the ideological gauge of his own intellectual history, and now Ienaga's energies were focused on demonstrating that that gauge was the fruition of the Japanese people's intellectual heritage." By identifying prewar roots of Japan's postwar constitution, Ienaga established a heritage for that constitution and protected it against claims (from the right) that the Americans had simply imposed it on a prostrate Japan. Ienaga's history-writing is a search in Japanese history for an awareness of the limitations of human activity—as in the thinking of Shōtoku Taishi, Shinran, and Uchimura; in the postwar years he transforms that early awareness into the cornerstone of a search through more recent times. Kuroha writes:

Ienaga history is scholarship on which Ienaga staked the self in its *shoshin*. He developed his textual positivism as a method of giving life to that self in its *shoshin*. And the ideological distinctiveness of that *shoshin* is the democratic principle that aspires fervently to respect for the autonomy of human nature. Given these things, the Ministry of Education's certification of Ienaga's high school text *A New History of Japan* was an infringement on that very principle of democracy, in the true sense of those words, *an attack on his person*. Thus, we should see the Ienaga lawsuits in response to that infringement, that attack, as the internal workings of Ienaga history.[14]

In this stunning summation, Kuroha links the three decades of Ienaga's life and scholarship (from 1935 to 1965) indissolubly with Ienaga's decision to sue the Ministry of Education. Biography is destiny, intellectual history becomes activism, and Ienaga hoists twentieth-century Japan on his shoulders as he attempts to embody in the late twentieth century the subjectivity, the modernity, the commitment to conscience whose existence he has sought to identify and trace in Japan's earlier history.

Japan has not been noted for its autobiographical writings. Occasional writing, diaries, and "pillow books," yes. Autobiographies, no. There has been no Cervantes, no Dag Hammarskjöld, no Johnson/Boswell. Ienaga is one of few twentieth-century historians to compose an autobiography. And there are fairly narrow limits within which Ienaga chooses to operate. We learn about his scholarly ideas and literary ambitions and his disappointments in these spheres. Ienaga tells us something about his birth family—quite a bit about his father but nothing about his mother (nor has he written of her elsewhere). He tells us virtually nothing about his wife. Indeed, we learn late in chapter 6 that in the final days of the war he left Tokyo for his wife's family home in the country, and that is the first mention of a wife! He attributes some of his new sensitivity on women's issues to an issue with his wife's family, but he refrains—here and elsewhere—from being more specific. We learn of no children. (Much later, in seeking a permanent site for his archive of materials relating to the textbook lawsuits, Ienaga writes in a private letter that no one in his family

---

14. Kuroha Kiyotaka, "Ienaga shigaku no konnichi ni yobikakeru mono," *Rekishi chiri kyōiku* (September 1965); pp. 1–8. Italics in original.

will take over, another tantalizing glimpse beyond the formal exterior. But it was the recipient of the letter, not Ienaga, who reported it.[15]) This reticence is less exceptional in Japan, perhaps, than in the United States today, but it helps to remember that Ienaga is a product of his era—he was born in 1913.

What Ienaga tells us instead is his family background (chapter 1), his early education (chapter 2), and memories of schooling in his teens (chapter 3); the "Copernican revolution" in his thinking (chapter 4); his life as a student at Tokyo Imperial University (chapter 5); and his career during the war (chapter 6). These chapters form 60 percent of the autobiography. The remaining chapters treat his life between the end of the war in 1945 and his retirement in 1977: his state of mind immediately after the war (chapter 7), the growth of his "social consciousness" (chapter 8), the experiences that led him to file the lawsuits (chapter 9), and, finally, the suits themselves and the struggle to defend Tokyo University of Education (chapter 10, written for the second edition, 1977).

Ienaga ends his autobiography:

> I was a lover of books with the modest ambition of leaving a single volume of academic research to the world when I died. Yet to my great surprise, the textbook suits and the fight to democratize Tokyo University of Education became my life's work. In each case I did little more than let myself be pulled along by the great abilities of many kindred souls, but I count it the glory of my life that I took part in activities "to defend intellectual freedom" that without doubt will live through all history. Not much time is left me, but I pray earnestly that I will hold to my convictions until my dying day.

He repeated this hope to me when we talked in 1993 in Tokyo. Ienaga has now survived this autobiography by nearly twenty-five years. We may lament the fact that Ienaga has spoken and written only occasionally about his life since 1976; in part to compensate for the fact that this autobiography ends twenty-five years ago, I have incorporated excerpts from these interviews and essays in insets scattered through the chapters of this translation. But there is an overarching unity to Ienaga's life since 1950. Ie-

---

15. Yamazumi Masami, "Kyōkasho saiban to *Nihon bunkashi*," *Geppō* 4, p. 2.

naga resisted what he considered the abuse of governmental authority and perhaps (to echo Kuroha) personal assault. He did not yield in the 1950s and 1960s and 1970s, years that he covers in this autobiography. In the years after 1976 he has carried on. He has not sold out. He has not forgotten his *shoshin*. Ienaga did not sell out but saw the suits through to their less than happy conclusion in the Supreme Court of Japan in 1997.

One of the lawyers who argued Ienaga's suits has offered his reading (1998) of Ienaga's character:

> One has to ask again what it was that set Professor Ienaga on a course of action that involved so much sacrifice, and indeed, one must imagine a depth and breadth beyond the grasp of the ordinary person in the personality, the character of the person who embarks on such a course—in terms of society, the qualifications of one conscientious citizen. I can't express it precisely, but it is not in some facet of a person, in some specific talent or qualification—be it historian or university professor—that Professor Ienaga excels but transcending those facets, in qualifications and talents as human being (or as total human being), or—changing focus slightly—as citizen of modern society.

Once the lawsuits ended, a junior colleague addressed the vacuum they left: "Ienaga's lawsuits have come to an end, but the attack on textbooks from the other side continues. . . . Come to think of it, while these lawsuits were in progress, we too relied on Ienaga for moral strength. From now on we have to figure out a new arrangement, how to do battle with these forces."[16] How the next generations shape that new posture is up to them, not up to Ienaga, but he has clearly done his part. In an interview of 1990 Ienaga spoke of the lawsuits as a " 'gift' to the next age, to the next generation":

> During the war I had my hands full protecting my own conscience; there wasn't any question of doing anything about the general situation. Yet at the time I didn't have any idea that even then there were people like Yanaihara Tadao and Masaki Hiroshi who carried out the will to resist even in those worst of times.

---

16. Kitajima Manji, *"Zadankai,"* in *Rekishi no hōtei,* p. 217.

After the war I came to write textbooks and mentioned these resisters in the footnotes. I wrote so the pupils could look back with pride that Japanese were not all bad, that there had been these people too, so that pupils would be able to accept this as a legacy of history.

As for the lawsuits, the aim was to win, but I thought that even if we were unable to win, there was meaning in the fight itself. In World War II among Japan's own Axis partners, for example, the Italian people rose up, and, particularly in the north, even conducted partisan warfare. In Germany, the Nazis didn't fall until the end, and the war ended with the destruction of the Nazis, but before then there were a great many people who resisted. Only in Japan was there no resistance. This fact determines the postwar situation, I think. The fact that the postwar era developed in this sleazy way—isn't it because we weren't able to fight enough during the war? If that is the case, the greatest gift we can leave for today's next generation is a "heritage of struggle."

It may be presumptuous of me to say so, but if the textbook lawsuits become a "gift" to the next age, to the next generation, I will deem it an honor.[17]

After the final verdict, in which the Supreme Court found in Ienaga's favor on several specifics but ruled against him on the issue of principle—that the Ministry has the right to certify textbooks—Ienaga received a telegram from his distinguished contemporary and colleague Maruyama Masao. Maruyama wrote that he foresaw victory for Ienaga "in the court of history." Maruyama is surely right that the court of history will render a far different verdict on the career and contributions of Ienaga Saburō.

Translated literally, the Japanese title of Ienaga's autobiography is "The Path One Historian Has Taken" or "The Steps of a Historian"—idiomatic in Japanese but less effective in English. So I have used the term *odyssey*. But I intend the term in the straightforward sense of journey or experiences or life. From Homer's *Odyssey*, the term often has the connotation of homecoming, of a return from a long sojourn abroad. That connotation is not appropriate here, for two reasons. First, Ienaga has never traveled outside Japan. His travels in Japan have been for the most part

17. Interview with Sawachi Hisae (January 20, 1990), *Taidanshū*, pp. 103–104.

in support of court cases, and he comments somewhere that he thought the example of Immanuel Kant, who never left his home town of Königsberg, a bit extreme. Second, the lives of some other Japanese intellectuals—for example, the writers Tanizaki Junichirō and Mishima Yukio, the constitutional scholars Hozumi Yatsuka and Uesugi Shinkichi—embody a pattern of sorts, of liberal younger years marked by interest in Europe and America, giving way to a conservative if not reactionary maturity marked by a focus on Japanese tradition and uniqueness. Ienaga breaks that mold, decisively. In his younger years his interest was in Japanese tradition; in his mature years he redefined that tradition to stress precisely the non-nativist elements, the universals that he saw as important for the future. And in his old age he has maintained those commitments—to universals, to conscience, to resistance to undue state authority. His has been a long journey, an odyssey. But he has not wound up back where he started.

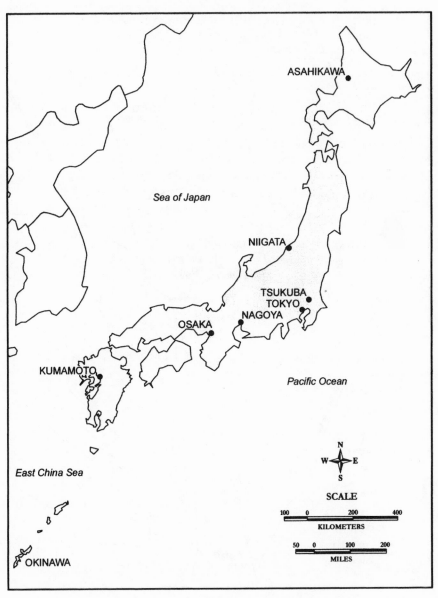

A map of Japan showing the major places of Ienaga's life and career.

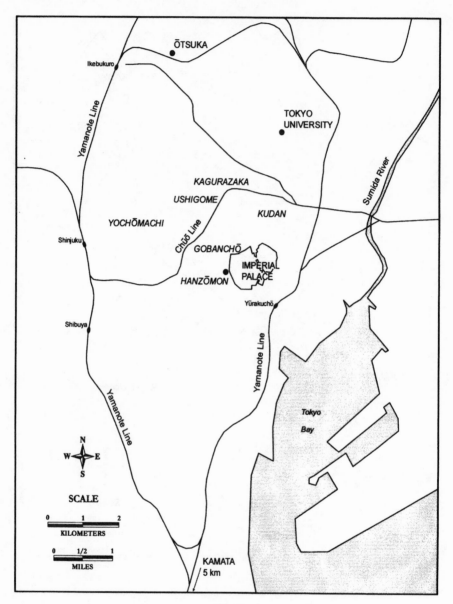

Tokyo

1

RECOLLECTIONS FROM INFANCY

It was in 1916 or 1917 that I first became aware of what was going on around me. My very earliest memories are of life in the house in Tamatsukuri, in Osaka's Higashi-ku. At that time my father was serving as commanding officer of Osaka's 17th infantry regiment. Before then we had lived in other places besides Tamatsukuri, but I have no memories of them; my memories begin with life in the Tamatsukuri house.

There was a shrine in the neighborhood, Sankō Shrine. Even today I still remember it: the main building on a high platform and beside the stone steps a pond with catfish in it. Some time ago, after forty-odd years, I went back to Tamatsukuri and searched for the shrine. The building had burned down during the war, but the steps I remembered and the stone lions were still there, and my eyes delighted in the sight.

I have no clear mental image of the area outside the house, but I have detailed recollections of the inside of the house, even down to the layout of the rooms; perhaps this is because as an infant I was kept cooped up indoors and hardly played outside. The house was a rented one—two of five row houses with the dividing wall knocked out, so there were lots of rooms. But there was no real garden, and right outside the living room was a high earthen wall, so we didn't get much sun. Living in such a house and not playing outdoors were not good for my health—of that, there can be no doubt.

For a time here Mother was confined to bed—tuberculosis, I think it was. Then for three months my invalid mother moved to Kaizuka, fifty miles south of Osaka, for her health, and she had to take me along. From the point of view of my health, the situation continued to be bad. I remember when I was still four or five complaining of a ringing in my ears and going periodically to the doctor. So my health was already cause for anxiety.

Here let me back up a bit and write of things that took place before I have memories of my own, things told to me later. I was born in Nagoya, on September 3, 1913, in Shirakabe-chō in Higashi-ku. At the time, Father was a lieutenant colonel in the infantry and serving with the Nagoya regiment; just before I was born, he was named commanding officer of Yatsushiro Division in Kumamoto [on the island of Kyushu], and I was born after Father had already set off alone for his new post. Some three months later the whole family moved to Father's new post in Yatsushiro—that explains why I have no memories at all of Nagoya.

While we lived in Yatsushiro, my older sister, who was going to primary school there, had to be admitted to the surgery of the hospital attached to Kyushu Imperial University in Fukuoka. So Mother accompanied her—with me, who was then nursing, strapped to her back. The three of us settled in for a long stay.

The hospital costs mounted, so Mother—who, of course, took over as nurse for my sister—had to cut down on her own expenditures for food, among other things. Under such conditions the mother's milk I received may not have amounted to full nourishment. Since infancy I have not been blessed with good health; it is at least conceivable that this stems in part from this time when I was still nursing.

As I say these things, you may wonder: How could an officer's household be so poor? Those who know only the days of the Pacific War, when officers cut fine figures, may think that to be an officer was to lead a life of luxury. But in my father's day the average officer—I can't speak of the officers attached to central headquarters—lived in unhappy circumstances that bore no comparison to the days when the military was at the height of its influence. In particular, 1915 and 1916, when I became aware of my surroundings, were a period of prosperity—World War I seemed about to end, and prices were rising, yet salaries were fixed, and our household had a very hard time of it.

The salary of a divisional commander in those days was barely 220 or 230 yen per month; taking various deductions into account, one's take-home pay sometimes dropped below 200 yen. In addition, there were other factors—for example, we had to send tuition money to my uncles, Father's younger brothers. Even

Photo 1.1   Ienaga's parents in 1900: Chiyo (mother, b. 1882) and Shintarō (father, b. 1873). Photo courtesy of Ienaga Saburō.

long afterward, Mother would often recall how rough things had been. At the time there were no bonuses for officers. The allowance for a divisional commander (the equivalent of today's expense account) was barely 20 yen a month. I remember that at New Year's the officers of the regiment would all gather upstairs and drink and make merry. Father simply could not hold his liquor, so while his fellow officers were having a high time, he would be in bed downstairs, already dead drunk. Thus the life of an officer, though at first glance splendid, was in fact a great financial burden for his family.

This inability to hold his liquor, combined with an awkwardness at personal relations, made Father's career all the more difficult. He was straitlaced, too, and apparently sometimes spoke bluntly to his superiors, in ways that ruffled their feathers. Even though he had graduated from the Military Staff College, he did not get along well with his superiors—perhaps for that reason, this Osaka regimental command was his last. In 1919, he received an honorary promotion (he was raised one grade and relieved of duty simultaneously), was put on the list of those awaiting assignment, and was then finally assigned to the reserves. As I said earlier, we had a lot of expenses, such as the hospital fees in the Yatsushiro period, and had even spent our savings from his years as major and lieutenant colonel, when, contrary to what one might expect, we were a bit better off. It was the worst of times: a fixed low salary in a boom period, with expenses swelling because as commander he had to keep up appearances and mix in society. It came as a great shock indeed when suddenly he lost his command. Looking back, it's hard to imagine, but he didn't get a lump-sum payment on retirement—not a penny. They gave him just the train fare home. Then after joining the reserves, he got only a slim pension; and because the two oldest of his four children were moving up to higher school, our household economy was in very tough shape.

From primary school on, I grew up as the son of a retired officer in hard times. For the sake of the children's health, Mother absolutely never ate eggs herself, yet invariably each morning she prepared an egg for me. I can't say I experienced true hardship, but I was acutely aware we were poor. In primary school my parents sometimes bought me a copy of *Boy's Life*, but I have no memory before fifth grade of their having bought an honest-togoodness book for me. It was barely possible to provide me with a magazine that cost less than 50 sen, but money to buy me real books costing more than one yen—in my family, that kind of money didn't exist. One time I heard a teacher at school mention a book called *The Tale of Ichitarō* and I told Mother that the teacher had said to buy it. Deceiving Mother, I got her to give me the money, and I remember buying the book, but even today I cannot forget her expression as she took the money from her purse.

This may not fall under the heading of poverty, but Father's was an Imperial appointment in name only, not in income, and we had to keep up middle-class appearances. Our chronic poverty continued, and this situation became an extremely important factor in shaping my character. When I was a sixth-grader, I think it was, I had to listen with a breaking heart as Father and Mother fought sharply about the inadequacy of the family income. My older brothers, off at the university and special higher school, were not often around, so they didn't know about such things. But I, being young, was home most of the time and grew up watching Father and Mother agonize constantly over how to make ends meet. From childhood onward I never thought rich people were happy, nor have I ever felt inferior for being poor; indeed, I have often taken pride in poverty. Why should that have been the case?

It happened, I think, when I was in third grade: for reasons of health, Mother sometimes cooked rice mixed with barley, and I intentionally said to a friend, the child of a well-to-do family, that I brought a lunch of barley and rice because we were poor. That friend seems to have thought I was serious. Even children must like to boast of honorable poverty. To be sure, my family's level of poverty was a long way from true poverty, so it is unlikely I had any consciousness of being a member of the unpropertied class. In the first place, Father was not a laborer. Among my classmates in fifth or sixth grade was H., the son of a streetcar conductor; thinking back, I seem to remember conduct that indicated he was class conscious, perhaps because of the influence of his father.

I had absolutely no such consciousness. We lived only a petit-bourgeois life, yet in later years I never had—nor do I have to this day—a consciousness of belonging to a specially privileged class. That may bear some relation to my home conditions when I was

young. In that sense, I was fortunate that the home of my youth
was not well off.

On this matter of the formation of a person's consciousness,
I came later to think, after I began to study intellectual history,
that we must give full weight to home conditions as a major factor. The historian Professor F., an acquaintance of roughly the
same generation as I, was born into the family of a Shinshū doctor, and how objective economic conditions influenced him was
precisely the opposite of how they affected pensioners' children
like me.

During the years of prosperity, we faced the gravest financial
hardship in my home; paradoxically, the depression years of the
late 1920s were a time when we had a comparative surplus. For
one thing—it may be a circumstance unique to my family—my
older brothers and sisters, far removed in age from me, were all
out of the nest and on their own; only I was still living with my
parents. In bad times prices fell, yet pensions remained fixed, so
pensioners were somewhat better off. Hence I have absolutely no
memories of the depression of the late 1920s. Later, after I began
to study history, I learned that extremely bad conditions developed in the villages—farmers selling their daughters, and so on—
but I myself did not experience the agony of the depression. That
fact indicates that objective social conditions do not govern an individual's life directly; instead, they affect individuals only
through the mediation of particular households.

I mentioned Professor F. a moment ago. His was the Shinshū
doctor's family, and while studying in Tokyo, he received money
from home. That source of funds was cut off, and he told me he
had a very tough time. His case is additional evidence that
changes in social conditions and the experiences of individuals
differ greatly according to people's home conditions.

Father started out on the high road to success, but he had to
leave his chosen profession at the young age of forty-seven. Why?
Because he was maladroit at getting along in the world—he was
unable to flatter his superiors and didn't master the worldly art of
getting along with peers. The result may have been financial distress for us, but I choose to look back with great respect for this
man who lived his life that way. Even had Father become a past
master of the art of social success and been promoted to lieutenant general and general, that success likely would not have meant

true happiness for us. Father did not shy away from bluntness, and as a result he occasionally met with disapproval from his superiors, but for me this is a matter of pride.

Father was born in 1873 and must have entered primary school about 1877. His place of birth was a village in the mountains, Yoshida in Saga Prefecture in northwestern Kyushu, a village with pottery as its chief product. In the 1920s his family led a life that was half-merchant and half-farmer (his parents harvested a very small quantity of rice). Judging from the fact that his parents couldn't afford to send Father past middle school, they were probably even poorer when he was young. Once long afterward Father told me of a passage in the primer he used in primary school: "God is the creator of heaven and earth; man is the master of all beings." The primer must have been a translation of one of the Western books used widely in early Meiji.

It was still an age of freedom of the press and freedom of choice, and the primary school textbooks of that time were often written by or translated by the best thinkers—they were books that enjoyed a broad audience in those days. Books like Fukuzawa Yukichi's *Conditions in the West*, Tsuda Shinichirō's *International Law*, Kanda Takahira's *On Law*, and Katō Hiroyuki's *Representative Government* were used as school texts.[1] In today's terms, these books were civics texts, and they incorporated fully the modern constitutional thought of the developed countries. To be sure, they translated Western theory literally, so it is very much in doubt whether everyday Japanese people, who had not yet awakened from the dreams of a feudal age, understood these difficult ideas clearly. It's hard especially to imagine how primary schoolers studied these difficult ideas. But the people of old were accustomed at an early age to "reading" the Four Books and Five Classics of the Confucian tradition, so perhaps the obstacles were not so great as we think. And though the books may have created some problems of comprehension, literal translations in their very literalness may have introduced the modern democratic spirit of Europe and American in its classic form, not, as in later years, bent by Japanese distortions like "Japanese-style democracy" or

---

1. Fukuzawa (1835–1901), Tsuda Shinichirō [Tsuda Mamichi] (1829–1903), Kanda Takahira (1830–1898), and Katō Hiroyuki (1836–1916): all were prominent educators, publicists, and translators of the early Meiji years, noted in part for their introduction of Western ideas.

"mimponshugi."[2] So the fact that these books had a wide audience—even if that audience did not understand them correctly—must have had some effect in spreading the spirit of modern democracy among the Japanese people.

Immediately following these years, the movement for liberty and people's rights welled up all over Japan, swelling indeed so that at one point it caused the authoritarian government deep anxiety. I think that fact is not unrelated to the content of early Meiji education. For that very reason, in 1880 the Meiji government, in a panic over the movement for people's rights, instituted policies controlling textbooks. Until then the system had allowed freedom of publication and freedom of choice; now the government prohibited the use of a number of books in the schools. All of the books I listed previously were ruled out at that time. In other words, this was the end of schools using textbooks that included ideas of democracy.

After that, Japanese education embarked on the road straight to nationalism. Father happened to enter primary school just before national control of education became a fact, and he used translated texts written in the spirit of Christianity—as in the passage he quoted me. This spirit of civilization and enlightenment of the early Meiji era probably had a great and lifelong impact on Father's thinking. One imagines military men to be hardcore believers in the Japanese spirit, yet Father's ideas—while utterly remote from so-called progressive ideas—were just as remote from divinely inspired Japanism. For one thing, Father was a confirmed materialist. He revered the Imperial House, but he didn't treat the emperor as a god. Reading newspaper accounts of a bill introduced into the Diet to clarify the national polity—this when Minobe Tatsukichi's formulation that the emperor was an organ of the state became an issue[3]—he said in disgust: "What in the world do they think they're doing?" Even today, his voice rings in my ears.

He flatly rejected all religions, quasi-religions, and superstitions; scoffed at horoscopes and geomancy; and to his dying day

2. *Mimponshugi* (literally, people-base-ism) is a concept developed by Yoshino Sakuzō (1878–1933). It contrasts with *minshushugi* (democracy; literally, people-head-ism) and seeks to reconcile imperial sovereignty and democratic goals.

3. Minobe Tatsukichi (1873–1948): scholar of constitutional law; author of emperor-organ theory; forced to resign from House of Peers in 1935.

held nothing resembling faith. As I shall relate later, he was hostile to socialism; still, upon hearing that the socialist Sakai Toshihiko[4] had a nonreligious funeral, he could not help sympathizing and let slip the comment: "I, too, should have a nonreligious funeral." To family members he repeatedly said that at funerals he liked short sutras and that when he died we should keep the ceremony and the scriptures as brief as possible; once he even said, "When I die, just heave my body in a ditch!" In addition, although a soldier, Father was critical of militarism.

In politics, he was a supporter of the Kenseikai (later the Minseitō) and critical of the Seiyūkai.[5] In part, this stemmed from an economic view that resonated with the Minseitō's fiscal restraint more than with the Seiyūkai's fiscal irresponsibility; in part, it related to the fact that he favored the Minseitō's policy of military cutbacks. At the time of the London Conference on arms reductions, when Katō Kanji, chief of the Naval General Staff, expressed stubborn opposition and was very much in the news,

---

Amaterasu Ōmikami is the distant ancestor of the present Emperor. Her power and virtue in their height and vast scale are like the brilliance of the sun. The Kōtai Shrine of Ise is the place where Ōmikami is worshipped.

The Great Japanese Empire is the land which Ōmikami gave Prince Ninigi to govern in the beginning. When Ōmikami sent the Prince down to this country, she gave an instruction, saying, "This country is the land where my descendants are to be rulers. You, my Imperial Grandson, go and rule it. The prosperity of the Imperial Throne, like Heaven and Earth, will endure for ever." The foundation of our country, which will continue for ever and ever, was actually laid at this time.

—Opening of textbook in use, 1911–1920

Source: Opening of Jinjō shōgaku: Nihon rekishi, the government-compiled text for elementary school students, in use 1911–1920; the translation is by John Caiger, in "Ienaga Saburō and the First Postwar Japanese History Textbook," Modern Asian Studies 3, no. 1 (1969): 16.

---

4. Sakai Toshihiko (1870–1933): founder of the Japan Socialist Party.
5. Kenseikai (Constitutional government association, 1916–1927); Minseitō (Rikken minseitō, People's government party, 1927–1940); Seiyūkai (Rikken seiyūkai, Friends of constitutional government party, 1900–1940): all major political parties.

Father was a firm supporter of the policies of the Hamaguchi Cabinet. He commented that there was no law that the navy minister had to go to the prime minister and criticize a treaty already concluded, that the role of the military was to take its assigned strength and figure out how to defend the nation; if they didn't like the treaty, they should resign.

During that time, the *Tōkyō Nichinichi* newspaper, to which we subscribed, occasionally ran essays by Tokutomi Sohō[6] advocating a positive foreign policy; Father denounced Tokutomi as a sunshine patriot. What a joke! At the time of the Sino-Japanese War, Tokutomi had supported the Portsmouth Treaty—the offices of his *Kokumin shimbun* were burned out on that account; but in more recent days he advocated a hard-line policy. Yet as time passed, from the China Incident to the Pacific War, Father's critical attitude gradually began to crumble. Completely sealed off from society, Father had no other means than the newspapers— then under complete government control—to judge the historical moment; it seems in retrospect that he had no alternative but to trust the military's propaganda. When negotiations between Japan and America came to a standstill, he grumbled that Japan's planes would have to ram American ships. Because I knew he had once been a supporter of international cooperation, I listened to these thoughts with sadness.

And I was sad, too, because of this memory. In 1929, when I was in junior high school, Ikezaki Tadataka had published a book entitled *Why Fear America?* I bought it and read it, and Father read it after me. At that time he was working temporarily for a company and brought home a clipping, a book review he had read at work in the *Asahi* newspaper, and gave it to me to read. It was a review by Mizuno Hironori, a captain in the Naval Reserves. Like the author Ikezaki, he didn't put great stock in America's military might, but unlike the author, he had great respect for America's economic power. Even if Japan succeeded temporarily in occupying Guam and the Philippines, Japan would win the battle but lose the war, so wouldn't war be simply a waste of young men's lives? Father thought the criticism very apt and gave me the clipping. Father must have had me read the review because he feared that I, reading the book, would fall prey to jingoism of the Ikezaki

---

6. Tokutomi Sohō (1863–1957): journalist and historian.

variety. In hindsight, Mizuno's review was insightful: it as much as predicted precisely the outcome of the Pacific War. Once Father had been impressed deeply with the review, but to me it was very sad that as the war progressed he came to voice such thoughts.

When the news came that Italy's Badoglio government had surrendered to the Allies, he commented, "They say they're surrendering for the sake of the nation, but it's really for their own sake." And although I tried to communicate—by wondering darkly how the war was going—the fact that there was no chance of victory, he replied that there was no alternative but to fight to the death. It may have been due to his military career that he couldn't conceive of surrender as a way out of the situation. Every time I think of Father's changed thinking during the war, I cannot but be struck by the thought of how strong the control of speech can be in determining a people's ideas.

As I mentioned earlier, Father was a supporter of the Minseitō; in that sense he was probably a capitalist liberal. So he was a firm and lifelong opponent of socialism. Just after the defeat, when labor unrest increased, he showed unhappiness at every incident. He was indignant at the plans for a general strike on February 1, 1946: "Outrageous!" To the end of his life he was utterly unable to understand the social movement and socialism. In my case, too, he was deeply concerned that I would be infected by socialism. I wonder whether his fear as a parent—that I would run afoul of the Peace Preservation Law [1925]—wasn't stronger than his ideological fear that his son would take to socialism. His real fear, I think, was of the threat of my arrest or detention under the Peace Preservation Law. In this sense, too, the Peace Preservation Law was able to exercise the utmost power to control "preventively" the people's ideas.

In discussing Father's ideas, I have drawn in part on recollections that come from a time when I had already formed my own intellectual position, so it isn't the case that all his ideas influenced me. Still, I was lucky that Father was not a fanatical Japanist.

2

EDUCATION IN THE PERIOD OF TAISHŌ
DEMOCRACY AND ITS EFFECTS ON ME

F ather was put on the retired list in 1919. When he left active
duty, he must have wanted to breathe the air of his native
place, and we moved to Karatsu, some thirty miles north of his
hometown in Saga Prefecture [Kyushu]. Father's older brother
was principal of an elementary school in a village less than three
miles away, so we had taken advantage of that connection and
moved to Karatsu.

I began school in Karatsu in April 1919, a first-grader. Back
then, the Karatsu school offered the compulsory six years and an
additional two or three years of middle-school training. The
school was situated in the precincts of the old Karatsu castle. In
a broad expanse of land surrounded by moats, the school had separate buildings and playgrounds for each class and a space where
the entire student body assembled. The buildings were large
enough that the classrooms, too, were large; behind the area
where the pupils sat was quite a bit of extra space. When I
changed schools, came to Tokyo, and found classrooms crammed
into corners and the only playground the size of a postage stamp,
I couldn't help staring in wonder, so great was the difference from
Karatsu.

The first-grade teacher in this school, in charge of my class,
was named Shibata Kiyo. Thinking back, I think she was still in
her twenties, a very strict teacher who often scolded her pupils.
But she was very fair: when two of us got into a fight, she always
punished impartially—even if one of the two was good, a model
pupil. To a child's mind, it was enormously impressive that she
was strict but fair. My conviction in later years that educators

39

must be fair stems, I think, from Shibata. But I remember little about the content of what she taught.

It is rather the natural beauty of Karatsu that even today awakens my fond memories. The coast of Karatsu was wonderfully scenic—the Ōshima peninsula jutting out into the ocean and, just offshore, two islands afloat on the water, the larger Takashima and the smaller Torishima. The town was also the terminus of the National Railway's Karatsu line, which ran through a field on the edge of town where we sometimes played. I had known only the squalid streets of Osaka, so this field with its milk vetch in bloom engraved itself on my soul; I won't forget it as long as I live. Sometimes even now, like a flash of lightning, that pastoral scene passes before my mind's eye. When I lie on my deathbed and review my life, it will likely be the scenic beauty of that field along the tracks, milk vetch in bloom, that will come back to me as the most beautiful memory of my life.

My older brothers soon had to go on to higher school, so we lived in Karatsu only a year and a half and then all moved to Tokyo. I transferred to Yochō-machi Primary School in Tokyo's Ushigome; there I was a second-grader. Okano Tarō, my new teacher, had a beard, and I was young, so he seemed like an older person; but as I think back now, he must have been in his twenties. He had just graduated from Aoyama Normal [teachers'] School and 1920 was right in the middle of "Taishō democracy,"[1] so the education we got had more than its share of striking characteristics. Okano declared that the ethics textbook was packed with worthless stuff, so it wasn't necessary to read it; we didn't even open it. Later, after becoming a professional historian, I looked at the civics text likely in use at that time—according to Karasawa Tomitarō's *History of Textbooks,* this was the third phase of textbooks that the government certified. The text did indeed contain lots of strange things. For example, at the beginning of the *Primary School Civics Text, Vol. 3,* for use in the third grade, there is the famous story of Ninomiya Sontoku,[2] spread across three chapters: "Filial Piety," "Diligence in Work," and "Study." The

---

1. Taishō democracy: the Taishō era (1912–1926) gave rise to the most liberal politics of prewar Japan; Taishō democracy generally denotes this period, which began in mid-Taishō and stretched over into the following Shōwa era.
2. Ninomiya Sontoku (1787–1856): paragon of Confucian virtues. His statue stood in every prewar schoolyard.

text states that as a child Ninomiya was poor, worked hard, was adopted into his uncle's house, and studied until late at night. Then it adds this conclusion: "At twenty Ninomiya returned to his own family, worked with all his might, and became a great man." There is no explanation of what "became a great man" means. At that time most Japanese had a low standard of living; and we can guess that the lesson here is for them: even if you're poor, you can become great, so don't get infected by dangerous thoughts that denounce the way society is organized. Furthermore, we can probably guess that part of the message is encouragement to make a success of yourself. The accompanying illustration shows a room with tattered *shōji*, a broken lamp, and a mother holding an infant son, with Ninomiya appearing concerned and helping. If you submitted it to today's textbook censors, the Ministry of Education itself would order it cut for being too gloomy!

In addition, this third volume has several chapters—the Ise Shrine, festivals, loyalty and patriotism, and the like—designed to foster "the national polity," and when you look at volume 4 (for the fourth grade), chapter 1 is "The Meiji Emperor," and with this opening it pushes the ideology of the emperor system: "The Meiji Emperor always treated his people as his children and shared their joys and sorrows." Chapter 5 is "Honor the Imperial House." It tells the story of how Toyotomi Hideyoshi[3] invited the emperor to his palace and had all the *daimyo* swear to honor the Imperial House. Chapter 24 is "Let's Obey the Laws" and reads as follows:

In ancient times the great Greek scholar Socrates did many things for his country and also taught the young men the right path. But Socrates was denounced by people who hated him, and in the end he was sentenced to death. His disciple Crito went to visit him in prison and urged him earnestly: "You haven't committed a crime, so there's no reason you must die. We can get you away, so please do escape." But Socrates replied calmly: "I have kept to the right path up till now for the sake of the country, so I can't go against it now. Better to uphold the laws of the country and die than break the laws of the country and live."

3. Toyotomi Hideyoshi (1537–1598): second of the three great unifiers of late sixteenth-century Japan.

That is the entire passage. What it is trying to say is no more or less than a moral injunction: even if you are condemned to death for a crime you did not commit, grin and bear it. Because it taught such ethics, education even during the age of Taishō democracy was formidable. Looking back, I think it was an excellent thing that Okano did not use the civics text.

Not only that, he said there was no need to buy the science text. Why not? Science was something to be studied through experiments and observation; reading a book was no way to study science. Here again, we have to concede that his idea was excellent. Okano explained to us second-graders the word *democracy*. It is because of memories like this that for me "Taishō democracy" is not simply a neutral historical label. To be sure, his definition included only the one aspect of equality before the law—that is, fairness and impartiality—and did not include the meaning of democracy; yet the fact that he taught the word *democracy* to second-graders tells us about the atmosphere of the times.

Or consider this. One time Okano turned to the pupils and asked, "Why are you kids going to school?" My friends gave various replies: that illiterate adults face hardships, that it is awkward not to be able to balance accounts, and the like. He summed them all up: "You're in school for your own sakes." I was a bit cocky, and I may have absorbed some of the nationalism of the time; I replied, "For the sake of Japan." Okano said that, too, was bad and finally indicated his own position. According to him, we were in school for the sake of the world, that if people the world over all studied hard and became wise, then they wouldn't make stupid wars any more and the world would be at peace. Looking back now, when the peace constitution has been established and world peace is touted as a national ideal, I can't help being deeply impressed by the fact that in the mid-1920s a teacher with this kind of spirit was teaching children.

Okano seems to have been a firm believer in the "Dalton Plan," popular at that time.[4] For a short time, he turned the desks around to have them all face in and tried to encourage us to teach ourselves. I don't know the real reason—whether this method was unjustly suspect as a means whereby teachers could in-

4. Dalton Plan: a more flexible approach (1920s) to class organization, named for the town of Dalton, Massachusetts.

troduce matters into the classroom under the rubric of self-instruction, or whether in fact it was an experiment—but it was stopped after only a few months. Either he didn't get the results he hoped for, or the principal told him to stop. We kids weren't privy to that, either. But in any case such experiments did take place. At the end of fifth grade Okano was transferred to the newly opened Tsurumaki grade school in the same Ushigome section of Tokyo, and when I was in sixth grade a friend of his, Oyama Uhachirō, came from another school to be our teacher.

Oyama is in good health even today—I saw him just recently after an interval of several decades; inquiring about various aspects of the school, I learned for the first time of the social standing of the school at that time, something we kids didn't understand. According to Oyama, our school at that time was famous, known like today's Banchō for attracting students from other districts. Hattori, who later became principal of Banchō, was appointed principal from among the ranks of those with degrees from normal schools; in accordance with his ideals, the school put into practice various new ideas. It was in that environment as well that Okano tried out his new teaching strategies. At the time we kids hadn't the slightest idea that our school was that special, so we didn't have a sense of its being different from other schools. As I look back, that was probably a good thing. Such education was probably possible precisely because it was that kind of school. And it was possible precisely because Tokyo's Ushigome was a progressive area. So one should not extrapolate from this one example to education in the nation as a whole.

As a matter of fact, at the same period we were getting this progressive education at our school, the exact opposite was taking place in areas outside Tokyo. In his *History of Textbooks,* Professor Karasawa gives details of the "Kawai Incident" that took place in 1924 in Nagano Prefecture, in the primary school attached to Matsumoto Women's Teachers College. These details of the incident are available in the October 1924 and March 1925 issues of the magazine *Shinano Education,* which Karasawa quotes. The gist is as follows:

> Miss Kawai, the intern, didn't use the prescribed texts for civics instruction but gave a talk based instead on Mori Ōgai's "The Revenge of Gojiingahara." That talk was like today's in-service training, and members of the examiners' committee

and many other visitors sat in and observed. In the evaluation that followed the session, the examiners' committee grilled Kawai on why she hadn't used the prescribed text. Kawai argued that she hadn't the confidence to teach the prescribed text. The examiners grilled her repeatedly: Which book did she take more seriously, the prescribed text or the Ōgai novel? Finally, they placed Kawai on furlough. What is more, her fellow intern Denda, having expressed unhappiness at this action of the authorities, likewise left the profession.

Even in the era of Taishō democracy—that most liberal period under the Meiji Constitution—primary school education was strictly controlled in this fashion by the national government. In Japan as a whole, the type of education I received was undoubtedly the exception of all exceptions.

Okano gave us this liberal education, but we got our history from the prescribed texts of the day. I'm not sure why, but Japanese history, and Japanese history alone—it began in fifth grade—was taught not by Okano but by a woman teacher. Whether Okano asked her because he didn't like giving the Japanese history class himself or for some other reason, I don't know; but we first learned Japanese history from *Primary School History of Japan,* the prescribed text of the day.

At the beginning of the text there was a four-page section: "Chart of the Imperial House." In order from Emperor Jimmu on down, it listed the emperors and their years on the throne. Then the text began: chapter 1, "Amaterasu Ōmikami"; chapter 2, "Emperor Jimmu"; chapter 3, "Prince Yamatotakeru"; chapter 4, "Empress Jingū"; and so on. Here is a bit at the start of chapter 1:

> The emperor's noble ancestor is Amaterasu Ōmikami. She had enormous merit and first caused rice and barley to be planted in the paddies and fields and silkworms to be cultivated, thus bestowing blessings on the people. Her younger brother was Prince Susanoo, and he occasionally acted wildly; but she always loved the Prince and did not reprove him. However, when the Prince defiled her weaving hall, she finally could not bear it and entered the heavenly rock-cave, closed the rock door, and hid inside. All the gods grieved on this account and, in order to get her to come out, gathered outside

the rock door and hung beads and a mirror on the branches of a sakaki tree and danced sacred dances. At that point Princess Amenouzume danced so comically that the laughter of the gods shook the earth. Wondering what was afoot, Amaterasu opened the rock door a bit, and saw herself reflected in the mirror that the gods had hung on the branch of the sakaki tree. Soon, strangely attracted, Amaterasu began to emerge from the door; Prince Tajikara, hidden at the side, grabbed her hand and pulled her out, and all the gods shouted with joy.

The tales went on and on: Susanoo descending to Izumo and subduing the eight-headed and eight-tailed dragon, Prince Ninigi's descent, and so on.

According to Professor Karasawa's research, in such fields as language the prescribed texts of the third period, compared with the textbooks of periods one and two (during Meiji), contained more teaching material of an internationalist nature and included some aspects that were quite liberal; but in history the third period saw a retrogression, and the legends that were mere sketches in periods one and two came to be written out at length, as in the previous passage. In chapter 2, "Emperor Jimmu," too, the progress of Jimmu from Hyūga until he entered Yamato was treated in great detail, including details about whether a giant crow led him to Yamato and whether a golden hawk rested on his bow. The chapter "Prince Yamatotakeru" contained illustrated stories of the conquest of the Kumaso and of how at Yaizu he waved his famous sword Kusanagi and cut his way through the plain that had been set on fire; the chapter on Empress Jingū covered the conquest of the kingdoms of Korea. Then came the story of Emperor Nintoku and the smoke and others like it, all of them from the *Kojiki* and *Nihonshoki*—accounts that, although not historical fact, were recounted verbatim as historical.

In this format, history, of course, had little room for objective facts such as how Stone Age man lived or the birth of Yayoi culture. Instead, history was buried under myths and legends that to the eyes of people educated after the war are unthinkable as history. Looking back, why—contrary to all common sense—did this book include myths, with no doubts expressed whatsoever as to their accuracy as history? I myself don't completely understand the psychology of the time, but I can say that none of my friends doubted they were factual.

Professor Karasawa tells of an incident that took place after 1935 in Ibaragi Prefecture. Seeing a scroll painting of Prince Ninigi's descent, a student said, "Teacher, that's a lie!" The teacher replied, "Are you a traitor? Shame on you!" and struck him with a wooden sword. But whatever the reason, we apparently didn't have even that much doubt. For the most part, so long at least as I was reading this text, I didn't find it strange; I accepted it. I remember how great my shock was when, immediately after entering middle school, I read Professor Nishimura Shinji's *Age of Yamato* and realized for the first time that the history I had learned at school was quite different from objective history. Reading a book like that, I was able relatively soon to move beyond the unscientific history taught in the schools; but most people, not having that opportunity, probably had no alternative but to carry what they had learned with them into adulthood. In fact, even today, twenty years after the war, quite a few people still rejoice at the revival of the festival of February 11 and believe that Emperor Jimmu was a real person; this is one telling index of how fearsome prewar education was.

Material like those that I have described appeared at the beginning of the Japanese history text. But what of the end, the most recent ages—how were they organized? This text was mainly organized around people, and a person's name always served as chapter title. At the end were chapter 51, "Emperor Meiji" and chapter 52, "The Reigning Emperor." Because I used this text in the Taishō era, "the reigning emperor" was the Taishō Emperor. The contents of the chapter "Emperor Meiji" were as follows: the Meiji Restoration, the Satsuma Rebellion, the Promulgation of the Constitution, the Sino-Japanese War, the Revision of the Treaties, the Russo-Japanese War, the Annexation of Korea, and the Death of the Emperor. "The Reigning Emperor" included only the accession of the emperor and Japan's involvement in World War I. For the most part, the chapter on Emperor Meiji mentioned domestic events until the promulgation of the constitution; thereafter, everything related to international affairs—the Sino-Japanese War, treaty revision, the Russo-Japanese War, and the annexation of Korea. And then at the end came the death of the emperor, an internal matter of the Imperial House.

The chapter on Emperor Taishō left out virtually all domestic political issues, and it treated only an internal Imperial House

> How great sacrifice and how long it took to escape from the after-effects of this educational pollution! When I think of it—even though the educational content of that time was not all bad, I get angry all over again at having had indoctrinated into us the anti-democratic, unscientific, militarist ways of thinking.
>
> —1986
>
> Source: Ienaga, "Gekidō shichijūnen no rekishi o ikite" (1986), in Ienaga Saburō shū, vol. 16, p. 261.

matter—the accession of the emperor—and international affairs, the Japanese actions against Germany during World War I. As for matters that occurred after the promulgation of the constitution in 1891, the text adopted the policy of teaching nothing at all about domestic political issues; that is the only conclusion one can reach. Mention the Taishō era now, and "Taishō democracy" is the first thing that comes to mind, and then the maturation of the capitalist economy, the development of the labor movement, the establishment of party politics, the advance of constitutional government. But the text includes not a line about any of that. This fact alone indicates how slanted history teaching was then. Insofar as the educational world was concerned, even the age of Taishō democracy marked no major difference from Meiji.

Be that as it may, on looking back I think I was most fortunate to have received that very important primary education in the era of Taishō democracy. Since then, I have been able to resist being engulfed by fanaticism, and that at least is attributable to my having gotten, at the start, an education that for all its limitations was the most liberal of the day.

3

DRAWN TO HISTORY: RECOLLECTIONS
OF MIDDLE SCHOOL

In March 1926 I graduated from Yochō-machi Primary School and in April entered First Tokyo Municipal Middle School. At that time thère were, I think, only seven or eight prefectural middle schools. The entrance examinations were pretty stiff, though not as stiff as they are today; in order to augment the prefectural middle schools, two municipal middle schools had been established, and they had opened two years earlier. I applied to one of those two new schools, First Tokyo, and luckily got in. I took a year off, so I graduated with the fourth class, but when I entered I was a student in the third class, and there were only two classes ahead of me—the second-year students and the third.

At the time, First Tokyo still had no buildings, so it rented space in a school outside Hanzōmon. First Tokyo didn't have fine facilities, but it did have the best possible location. It looked out on the moat at the Hanzōmon entrance to the palace; just behind the school yard was the interior moat, and the green palace trees were right before our eyes. It was scenery otherwise not to be found in Tokyo; there were even pheasants. Still, because we faced the moat, the palace police kept a sharp eye out, and if we climbed down into the moat to retrieve a ball that had fallen in or did anything like that, they were quick to reprimand us. The streetcar road where the British Embassy was located was called Goban-chō (the streetcars don't run there any more, and the street has been renamed Samban-chō); in spring, the cherry blossoms came into full flower on both sides of the street, and we sometimes had military drills under the cherry trees. In all Tokyo there can't have been another school with so scenic a location. I

49

was there for only one year, but starting middle school in such a place left me with memories I will never forget.

The first principal of the school was Narita Senri, who after the war became chair of the Tokyo School Committee. Narita knew his own mind, and in education, too, he had his own ideas. Politically, his mindset had its extremely conservative—indeed, reactionary—aspects, as I will relate later. Thinking about it today, I find many of his opinions impossible to agree with, but still I cannot help thinking highly of him, if only because he had a strong and positive desire to demolish received notions. For example, middle-school students at the time all had to wear a school uniform—a jacket with a high collar, buttoned up in front. Narita thought these jackets were not good for our health, so both municipal middle schools chose instead a suit and black necktie. And because in his view over-the-shoulder satchels were also not good for our health, he made us carry knapsacks. Going back and forth to school wearing a suit and carrying a knapsack was a real break with the middle-school customs of the day, and we couldn't help noticing that people stared at us.

I entered school before the use of knapsacks had been ordained, so on the pretext that I had a satchel I had already bought, I got by without having to use a knapsack, but I remember feeling a slight sense of shame each time I went to school wearing a suit. Sometimes on streetcars we were mistaken for conductors! Narita apparently got the idea of suits from student apparel at England's Eton and Harrow. Alongside the extreme nationalism in his thinking was also, undeniably, a tinge of Anglophilism. I remember that the names Eton and Harrow cropped up again and again in his speeches as principal.

Narita also had a great competitive urge, and he always wanted to be Number One in everything. One indication of this is that the school's name was not Tokyo First Middle School (as in the Tokyo First Middle School established by the prefecture), but First Tokyo Middle School—"First" coming first. The city's Second and Third middle schools, established later, did not follow this practice, so it was First Tokyo flattering itself; still, its high ambition gave us students an exhilarated feeling.

Narita's unique educational ideals made themselves apparent in various ways. For example, during summer vacation he took the entire student body to a hostel in Chiba Prefecture,

Photo 3.1   Ienaga Saburō in middle-school uniform, 1928.
Photo courtesy of Ienaga Saburō.

where we lived together dormitory-style. In winter he even made us swim. He did have a rather violent streak. One time in a P.T.A. meeting, a parent expressed concern that swimming in winter was bad for the weak, and he replied, irresponsibly, that if a student couldn't take it, it wouldn't matter if he died. Still, in the educational world of the day, there was already a strong tendency to push people on to higher schooling—"The exams! The exams!" Even today I think he was right in trying to give students an education in the broader sense of the term, not one focusing solely on academics.

The way he conducted school excursions, too, was really advanced for middle schools. They weren't like school excursions nowadays, trips that are half-pleasure: rent a bus and tour only famous spots, leaving everything up to the tour company. First, geography and history guidebooks Narita had written were distributed, and each student was assigned a research topic concerning a specific site along the way; before departure, a session was held at which the students themselves reported; and even during the trip the students always had maps in hand and were made to study carefully the history and geography of the places we visited; after we got home, we had to present a detailed report. Even today's college students might not be up to this kind of excursion. I think you can see the special character of First Tokyo's instruction from the simple fact that it did such things with middle-schoolers.

There were also lots of extracurricular activities. Theater, for example: in the lecture hall of the new building at Kudan, completed in 1927, we put on such period pieces as *Daibosatsu tōge*, complete with floodlights, wigs, and genuine swords.[1] I took virtually no part in such extracurricular activities, but once, when I was helping out backstage with the props or something, the physical education teacher came by and joked, "Only lady-killers back here!" That teacher was really ugly, so one friend whispered to me—I remember it still—that compared to him, anyone else was a lady-killer. But such extracurricular activities were a great boon to middle-school life.

Already at that time, such places as the prefecture's Fourth Middle School, predecessor of today's Toyama High School, focused on preparing students for entrance examinations to higher school. Fourth Middle was then near the outer moat in Ushigome Mitsuke. There were boats for rent in the outer moat, and there were tales—I haven't checked to see whether they were true—of students having been expelled for going boating after school. The students simply didn't do extracurricular activities. Later, after

---

1. *Daibosatsu tōge:* play by Yukitomo Rifū, based on novel by Nakazato Kaizan (1885–1944). It premiered in 1921 and became a classic in the *Shinkokugeki* (New National Theater) repertory.

Human history is the history of the great majority of people. A minority of power-holders or heroes or a few intellectuals—they aren't what moves history forward. History is constructed through the collective efforts of the many, the nameless. Japanese society is very slow-moving, and we cannot deny that its reforms have often been incomplete, but that people's status has improved one step at a time is a fact running through the key points of our history. In order to make that clear [in my textbook], on the opening page at the beginning of each age, I present photographs with the caption: "People behind historical progress." And at the same time, the realm of culture is not, as before it often was, the culture only of the ruling classes; there is rich culture among the people, too, and it is not simply a culture that supports the existing order, but all sorts of ideas and culture to change the existing order have arisen in Japanese history, and we need to know that and must have the self-confidence to move history ahead in a forward-looking direction.

Our heritage includes the efforts of many individuals among our ancestors to move Japanese society forward. The prewar historical education covered all this up. It's highly embarrassing that for a long time people like me didn't know these facts, so I wanted to transmit as much as possible of that supreme cultural inheritance, spiritual inheritance of our ancestors, so as not to bequeath to the next generation, once more, my own mortification.

—Court testimony, 1969

Source: Statement under direct examination, Tokyo District Court, Civil Court 2 (Judge Sugimoto presiding), July 12, 1969; in *Shōgenshū*, pp. 132–133.

enrolling in higher school, I checked with graduates of Fourth Middle and found that to be the case. The prefecture's First Middle, predecessor of today's Hibiya High School, was just as famous as Fourth Middle for being a cram school, though I understand it wasn't quite so bad. But First Tokyo was very different.

To be sure, one consequence was that its record for getting people into higher school wasn't so hot, and among my classmates only a very few succeeded in getting admitted to higher school "straight," right after year four. Nevertheless, I think it offered a highly desirable middle-school education: it did not put excessive pressure on us—"The exams! The exams!"—and we could enjoy various extracurricular activities to the fullest.

I took practically no part in extracurricular activities. Physically, I was severely limited. I've already mentioned that as an infant I had to accompany my older sister and live a hospital life. In 1923 my younger brother developed tuberculosis and that summer moved to the village of Hayama on the sea. Then, in September the Great Earthquake made the house in Ushigome unlivable, and Mother took me to live in a rented house in Hayama so that she could attend to my brother.

I went to the Second Primary School in Hayama until March of the following year. In April we moved to Tokyo, and I changed schools once again, to Yochō-machi; the next year I contracted an inflammation of the lymph glands in the lining of my lungs. Since infancy, it had been my fate always to have to keep company with sick people; now, it seemed, I suffered the gravest consequences of life at Hayama. From time to time after entering First Tokyo, I would run fevers; soon I was diagnosed as having pleurisy. At that point I resolved to take a year's leave from school for medical treatment, so I recovered completely, but that sickness in my lungs left in my body the seeds of lifelong and ineradicable future trouble. Of course, by contracting the disease at an early age, I gained immunity, so I was not in danger of contracting tuberculosis later, but thereafter if I got slightly tired, I remember a dull pain in my upper body and an indescribable and disagreeable feeling in my whole body, while sometimes I ran a continual slight fever. I am not a medical specialist, and it is difficult for me to say whether I developed these problems because of the legacy of my past or because of my gradually worsening stomach and intestines; still, no matter what the cause, because of illness at the time I graduated from primary school and entered middle school, my health deteriorated greatly.

What is more, since infancy my digestion had not been good. It embarrasses me to talk of indelicate things, but I have one memory of a primary school excursion on which I suddenly needed to go to the bathroom while on the streetcar; I had to get off all by myself, use the station toilet, and then take the next streetcar. From about the time I entered the university I began to display symptoms of permanent and chronic digestive ailment, and down to the present day—decades later—I still have not entirely recovered. The specialists agree that I probably won't ever get better.

All the guests [at a banquet in 1960] were really digging in, and amid them Ienaga stood out because he was eating like a bird. To my impolite question, "Why aren't you eating?" he replied something like, "Chronic gastritis." Back then Ienaga always sat on the tatami with his back straight as a ramrod. I thought the word "stoic" described him precisely.

He awes me: with that small thin frame—"delicate" fit him perfectly—he fought the long textbook lawsuits through to their conclusion, and even today he is in good shape. . . . It's probably his gift of extraordinary strength of spirit, but from his youth he has made a habit of rubbing himself down with a cold wet towel, and before going to bed he does his own regimen of stretching exercises to keep limber—something beyond me. He has said that reading is his only hobby, that he dislikes tobacco and alcohol, and that to save time he forgoes pleasures.

—*Lawyer, 1998*

Source: Shimomura Sachio, "Kimajime de stoikku na sensei," in *Geppō* 5 (March 1998): 5–6.

Moreover, since infancy I have suffered from nerves; even in primary school I suffered from insomnia. It started with my being unable to fall asleep; afterward, I couldn't sleep late. After going to bed I would take several hours to fall asleep; occasionally, I'd go all night without sleeping a wink. Also, my nasal passages weren't straight, so all year round they got congested, and that was another cause of sleeplessness. And from the time of primary school I had strong myopia; by fifth grade I couldn't see the blackboard without glasses. Thus, virtually my entire body had problems. Only my ears and my legs were sound. So I'm not exaggerating when I say my whole life has been a struggle against physical ailments.

For me physically, hardly a day passed that was completely without pain. At my heaviest as a young man, I weighed ninety-nine pounds, and in the postwar era my weight sank to about ninety pounds. In the last twenty years, my daily consumption of food has never exceeded two or three slices of bread and a third of a pint of rice. Perhaps because I eat and drink so little, my blood pressure is extremely low, and the slightest effort leaves me exhausted; when I overwork, I don't recover easily, even with rest. So I have to get as much rest as I can; I can spare virtually no time for pleasure. Unlike normal healthy people, to preserve my state of health I have to have time in which to do nothing, to float, to rest. Consequently, I can't think in an active sense of pursuing pleasures but must live with my supreme goal being the negative one of freeing myself even a bit from physical pain. The role my physical condition has played in the formation of my ideas is a topic I will have occasion to address later, but having to restrict to the greatest possible degree the expenditure of energy on matters not absolutely essential meant I developed a passive attitude toward life. Already in middle-school days, this attitude may have been evident in my tendency to stay a semi-invalid, to take virtually no part, for example, in extracurricular activities.

Still, the fact that I took a year's sick leave soon after entering middle school was not necessarily a complete minus. I attended school only one semester before taking the year off, so as far as English and other subjects that began in middle school were concerned, it meant that I left after completing only the introductory material. So when I repeated the courses the following spring, I started from scratch once again; in terms of preparing me for later study, that was a major plus. I really wasn't smart, so in English, math, and the other courses that were new at middle-school level, I had sat there, stumped, not really understanding them. Then I was lucky enough to have the opportunity to do everything over again several months later, so from that point on I was able to pursue my studies without major difficulties. Based on this experience, I really do want to say that for young people, a slight delay of one or two years, viewed in the context of an entire life, is not necessarily a significant minus but may even be a major plus. Of course, one might say that my abilities were deficient, in that I needed this kind of review, and that I was apparently sort of handicapped mentally, unable to do what normal people could.

Since my primary school days I have always been particularly poor at mathematics—called arithmetic in the primary school curriculum of the day. Even today I can't use an abacus at all and am poor at doing sums in my head, to the extent that in stores I often miscalculate the change I'm due. Moreover, I'm not good with my hands, so I was very clumsy at manual arts, which then went by the name of crafts. And then my motor nerves were not developed—it makes more sense to say that physically I was completely hopeless, so gymnastics was the thing I hated most. On days we had gym, my gloom settled in the day before. I might just as well say it: I was totally unable to do vaulting and the other exercises. Even now I can't catch a ball thrown my way.

I managed to make it through primary school that way, but when I entered middle school, I faced—as I have already mentioned—Narita's concept of education, unique and very strenuous. If one didn't take part, so it was stated, one couldn't graduate. But I took a leave of absence for illness immediately after entering, and on that pretext I was able to get special treatment that exempted me all the way through from all courses and functions related to physical education. I didn't take part in the summer or winter conditioning in the dormitory in Chiba Prefecture. Even today I find it strange that they let me graduate. Hence, I'm not really a First Tokyo graduate in the full sense of the word. Perhaps they let me graduate out of pity. But from primary school days on, I had been good at writing. Untalented as I was, I had only one salvation: I loved to write. I loved to write, but in the very first days of primary school, I really didn't express ideas that came welling up from inside me. Rather, I had been a very early bloomer only where reading was concerned, and instead of children's books, I began to read what the grown-ups read and be-

---

As a result of many conditions, during the war I immersed myself wholly in the world of religion that transcends this world and barely escaped jumping on the bandwagon of the war, but I was unable to criticize it head-on.

Shōtoku Taishi said: "This world is empty, only the Buddha is true."* The things of this world are all relative; they have no absolute meaning. By relativing the actual, I could keep my distance from the state and particularly the storm of fascism that raged so wildly. At the same time, via these teachings of Buddhism, I approached the Bible, too, and was impressed very greatly with its words: "Our citizenship is in Heaven."

—Court testimony, 1969

Source: Statement under direct examination, Tokyo District Court, Civil Court 2 (Judge Sugimoto presiding), July 12, 1969; in *Shōgenshū*, pp. 112–113.

*Shōtoku Taishi (Prince Shōtoku, 574–622): regent from 594 to 622, author of 17-Article Constitution (604).

came adept at writing sentences too difficult for most children to write, so it was simply that I shocked my teachers by writing very pedantic prose. But since I lacked confidence in all other subjects, composition gave me my only hours of pleasure.

Even after entering middle school, I took absolutely no part in extracurricular sports; similarly, in drama and music and the like, I did not step forward. But the school magazine was a different matter: from year one onward, I submitted a lot of writing. In my second first year—that is, after my year off—I submitted an essay that aped scholarly writing, although it is an exaggeration to call it an essay. It was entitled "The Ancestors of the Japanese People," and the geographer Asai Jihei (who is still in good health and pressing on with his research) praised my work. In reality this essay was little more than a précis of Nishimura Shinji's *Age of Yamato*, which I read about then and which greatly impressed me; from that time onward I was interested in this subject, and that may have been an early clue to the direction my scholarly life was to take.

From the end of primary school, I loved reading the works of Natsume Sōseki and Shimazaki Tōson.[2] I started with Sōseki's *Botchan* and stopped at about *Pillow of Grass*. His real achievements—*And Then, Mon, Kokoro, Light and Shadow*, and the like—were over my head. Sōseki's writings were my first, eye-opening introduction to genuine classics. After entering middle school, I was deeply moved by the poetry of Shimazaki Tōson's youth. I have a strong sentimental streak, and even now I cannot get away from it: let me see an absolutely run-of-the-mill drama, and I immediately start crying. And so in Tōson's *Young Leaves* I fell head over heels in love with the supremely smooth poems. For example:

> The path of dreams that maidens take
> now lies behind me, most of it.
> When I look back on this, my world,
> fair hills I see, and rivers, too:
>
> Alongside River Edo's banks,
> by quiet currents was I born,
> reached maidenhood beneath the shade
> of cherry blossoms on its shores.

---

2. Natsume Sōseki (1876–1916): author, scholar of English literature. Shimazaki Tōson (1872–1943): poet, novelist.

So many dreams have I now dreamed
in grass of spring, with daisies laced,
along the stream that flows into
the river broad where mallards float.

I was good at imitation, so I began to compose poems imitating this new-style poetry. In my four years of middle school I must have composed more than thirty, but unfortunately I've lost most of them. I have at hand two I composed in my fourth year, from the October 1930 issue of the school magazine; I offer them here for your amusement. The first is called "Ode to Moonlight" and goes as follows:

The clouds do tower high, so high
in ev'ning sky; now breaking through
the rays of light on ocean shine,
and shatter, all, upon the waves.

This light—perchance is it the Truth
that sacred sutras do proclaim?
The poets sing of how it turns
the world to silver—this moonlight.

In spring it shines on sleeping woods
and turns the trees to cloth of white;
transforms the flowers into frost,
afloat in fragrance—this moonlight.

In summ'r it shines upon each grain
of sand of ocean, great and wild.
Am I awake? or do I dream?
It speaks with pinetrees—this moonlight.

In fall it sheds its gentle rays
on fine brocade of mountain streams
and stills the oars of those who go
in small boats fishing—this moonlight.

O Moon, Thy rays shine down upon
the wife, who now at window sits,
with longing filled for husband dear,
departed on a journey far.

O Moon, Thy rays shine down on those,
whose breasts brim o'er with sadness great
as in the flute's so plaintive sound
they lose themselves—completely gone.

How many thousand years' laments
hast Thou lent sympathetic ear?
How many tens of thousand joys
of poets hast Thou hearkened to?

Thou shinest too upon the one
who naught but cries, most bitterly;
his clothes he clutches to his breast—
on autumn nights of exile drear.

Once, long ago, a chief of state
his own good fortune boasted of,
even compared himself with thee;
where is it now, his dream so bold?

Humanity has boundless hopes,
but life in truth has limits close;
we looking up at Thee do change,
but surely Thou art evermore.

The maiden's youth and beauty—Ah,
how long indeed will they endure?
The crimson flowers of this field—
how long before their colors fade?

This world is home to many; still
this silent beach knows none save I.
The tears I cry no one can see
as I stand gazing up at Thee.

In all creation, only one—
this moonlight shining down on me.
My dreams mayhap will not come true;
but I have eyes alone for Thee.

The second poem, "Midsummer's Dream," goes as follows:

In blackest shade of em'rald trees,
cicadas cry, then pause for breath.

The wind the fragrant young leaves stirs;
I lose myself in dream so deep.

I spread my silver wings out wide,
and see, below, the hills and streams;
the winged horse of Heaven, I
traverse the vasty firmament.

The sound of wings—how wonderful!
The woods, the fields go rushing by
as I peer down on changing world—
ten thousand leagues, this heav'nly trip.

My eyes cast wide, I do espy
my native place, afar off now
past purple meadows far beyond
'neath crimson clouds at eventide.

I gazed up once at mountains high,
their peaks capped with the snows of yore;
yet now those tow'ring mountaintops—
they too are far below my wings.

Were I to stand upon the beach,
the sea would surely fill my eyes;
now underneath my hooves I see,
so truly without bounds, the waves.

The bell-like sound—the wind's own voice,
the fragrant haze of evening,
the rainbow's varicolored arc
are zenith point of Nature's art.

The clouds, they rise up—suddenly
a storm disrupts the ev'ning sky.
My silver wings—they fall away;
in briny deep sinks Heaven's steed.

Ideals—eternal, like the stars,
are not like flow'rs, ephemeral;
those with eyes for flow'r of peach
know little of eternity.

Reading these two poems now, I think we can say the following about me as I was then. First, I was utterly immune to the fads of the day and was influenced greatly by a classic that was then out of fashion. I'm not an expert in the literary history of those years; still, it is certain that the poetry of those years was not so old-fashioned but more modern, largely in the language of everyday life. Yet I was influenced by the classical meter of Tōson, which took the world of the late nineteenth century by storm, and in the 1920s I prided myself on composing poems in this outdated style. Later, too, I experienced the same thing again and again in changes in my thinking: rather than the ideas of the day, the piping hot fads of the day, I was always influenced more by the old ideas of the era just passed, after a good bit of time had elapsed. My inability to follow the fashion of the day is, I think, a reflection of my stodginess. But for that very reason I was not influenced during the war by the militarism that was the fashion and clung instead to "anachronistic" liberalism, so I was able to avoid shameful opportunism. This very stodginess, not being able to respond immediately to the mood of the day, was not entirely a minus—again the reverse of what you would expect.

Second, as you've seen from reading them, my poems are merely an assemblage of beautiful words; they don't involve serious thought. At the time I was satisfied with this rhetoric, this romanticism; I had yet to undergo any intellectual angst.

As I have been saying, life at First Tokyo allowed enough leeway that I could not be hounded into an exams-at-all-costs mentality, but it was still intellectually a void. In school, one or two teachers seemed to have been influenced by the social currents of the time, by left-wing thought. One time there was a slightly leftist tendency in the play a science teacher put on for a class day, and it came under sharp criticism from the principal and the other school officials. I remember a lead essay in the school magazine in which Principal Narita emphasized that it was very dangerous in one's middle-school years to lose oneself in philosophy or literature, so it was safer to specialize in the more empirical sciences. Looking back now, I think the essay set forth a very frank educational philosophy that sought to prevent middle-school students from having a philosophical or social viewpoint and to immure them in technical studies in the natural sciences. I didn't have the perspicacity to see it then, but the principal did lean in that direction, so even though the school offered an education with some leeway, there was absolutely no chance that our eyes might be opened intellectually.

In history and ethics classes, too, what we got was education according to textbooks that had passed official scrutiny, and although these books didn't go out of their way to indoctrinate us in nationalist ideology, they didn't give us a chance to find a way of thinking that could break out of it, either. So from primary school until the spring of 1931, when I left middle school, the emperor system and its orthodoxy in pure form were instilled in me, and I was virtually unable to level any criticism at it. In that sense, we must recognize that even First Tokyo's education had severe historical limits. In such conditions I couldn't discover new intellectual issues; I could only devote myself as a literary adolescent to romanticism and romantic rhetoric and immerse myself in the self-satisfaction of publishing such poems, one after another, in the school magazine.

Third, my being imbued with the vice—if it is a vice—of wanting to see my writing in print began with my submissions to this magazine. By now I have seen my work in print hundreds of times—so many times even I can't arrive at an accurate count, but my experience of joy on setting my own writings into print began with my submissions to this magazine. So, the content of the writings aside, the extracurricular activities of First Tokyo did play a decisive role in my intellectual life after all.

Fourth, in the two poems I reproduced here, my awareness of human limits—this is, of course, hindsight, and it may be forcing a connection—comes relatively consciously to the fore. As I have already said, at the time I had not experienced any intellectual angst at all or confronted any issues, so what passes for thought in those poems comes not from cogitation but from the imitation of some classic. Still, as the later *Logic of Negation in Japanese Intellectual History* shows, my problem-consciousness is already present, albeit perhaps without my realizing it: the awareness of human limits and the recapturing of limitlessness by overcoming those limits. There is, I think, some significance to be found in that fact.

As for subject matter, in middle school my likes and dislikes became yet more pronounced. I was basically no good at arithmetic, and after entering middle school I became a student of the

> What historians write always becomes a crude sketch. That may be okay in broad terms, but it tends to be very formulaic—summing things up with terms like "imperialistic war." The work of getting into the details . . . and reliving that experience from the inside . . . or of digging into one tiny aspect, even using computers: there is a jigsaw puzzle that we call history, and it's enough if we're able, among the hundreds and thousands of pieces, to fix one or two for good. Later generations may finish the whole puzzle, but I think it's enough if we've fixed one or two useful pieces.
> —Interview, 1990
>
> Source: Interview with Sawachi Hisae, Taidanshū, p. 101.

liberal arts for good. I was good at composition, history, and similar subjects; but mathematics and science—physics and chemistry, in particular—always made me weep tears of frustration. I became fond of history, and therein lay a special karma from my infancy. When I was small, Mother often read me stories of Kusunoki Masatsura and the like,[3] so from the time I was an infant I had a special interest in history. Even before I began to go to school, I loved to look at the reference book my older sister used in her primary school history; it had appendices presenting historical conditions in pictorial form. Even in primary school my favorite subjects were composition and history, and by the time I entered middle school, I knew I wanted to be a historian. In the earlier years of primary school, I was, of course, good at composition, and we didn't have history until the fourth year, so about the third year of primary school I compiled all by myself a collection of nursery tales, and the children's edition of the daily newspaper Yorozu chōhō carried an article about me. The person in charge was Okano, and the paper printed his comment: "Ienaga is saying he will soon be a writer." Indeed, I really wanted to be a novelist. To tell the truth, even today I'd like to try my hand at writing a novel, and to the extent that I have gotten so far as the

---

3. Kusunoki Masatsura, son of Kusunoki Masashige (fourteenth-century warrior and loyalist). Their parting, in 1336 when the son was said to be ten, was a highly popular episode, omnipresent in elementary school textbooks and in a patriotic song later outlawed by the U.S. Occupation.

draft—no more—of the plot of a novel, even today I'd like to try. So it's not unnatural that as a child I wanted to be a novelist.

However, after becoming a middle-schooler, I realized that any thought of becoming a writer was a delusion, so I soon switched to wanting to become a historian. At about the time I entered middle school, I fell in love with *An Insider's Japanese History* by Shimbō Iwatsugu and learned a lot. This book was pretty advanced: it was written in formal and stilted prose, and many passages were paraphrased from classical sources. But I was ahead of my age group, and for me it was the ideal reading matter. I learned all sorts of information; even today, when I earn my keep as a specialist in Japanese history, some of what I learned from *An Insider's Japanese History* still sticks with me. What we read in childhood has enormous influence, and this is one example.

My interest in history tended solely in the direction of narrative history; Mother's sensibility and the impact of this book both played a role in that. But then my interest turned gradually in the direction of political history. To be sure, it was narrative political history, not political history in the elevated sense of the term we use today. About that time Tokutomi Sohō published the volumes in *The History of the Japanese People in Medieval Times* that dealt with Oda Nobunaga, Toyotomi Hideyoshi, and Tokugawa Ieyasu. I bought these volumes at the then-pretty-steep price of three yen per volume and was keenly interested in the battle of Sekigahara, the Osaka campaign, and the other battles; I even went on to the General Staff's *Battle History of Japan*. Along with these books, two others had an extraordinary impact on my intellectual life. One was Nishimura Shinji's *Age of Yamato*. And H. G. Wells's *The Outline of History* happened to appear about then, translated by Kitagawa Saburō under the title *Outline of World Cultural History*. Reading these two books caused a great change in my view of history.

Wells's history of world culture begins first with the creation of the universe and then proceeds in this order: the creation of the earth, the evolution of plants and animals, the evolution of man and of culture. Nishimura's *Age of Yamato* follows that form precisely, beginning with the creation of the universe and the evolution of humans and then proceeding to Japan of the Jōmon era and the establishment of the Japanese state. *An Insider's History of Japan*, my previous favorite, was written in the same way as the approved texts of the time: it began with tales of the age of the gods and—with the exception of the tomb culture—left the findings of archaeology out entirely. At the stage where I was when I read *An Insider's History of Japan,* I was unable to move beyond the approved textbook view of history, but in reading *The Age of Yamato,* I learned for the first time that history had to begin not with tales of the gods but with life in the Stone Age. Nishimura cited Tsuda Sōkichi's critical studies of the *Kojiki* and *Nihongi,* but I hadn't read any of Tsuda's works, so I couldn't understand the essence of the *Kojiki* and *Nihongi* as thoroughly as Tsuda's studies.[4] However, I did learn at least this for the first time: that the Japanese history that began with Amaterasu Ōmikami, as taught in the schools, was not objective Japanese history. Here I was, a first-year student in middle school and able already to grasp the origins of history in its scientific sense: that was my great good fortune.

But I knew only that the tales of the age of the gods were not objective historical fact; at that stage I didn't have anything approaching a full-fledged critique of the ethical ideas of the national-polity school, which took the tales of the age of the gods as its ideological base and was built solidly atop them. The orthodox national morality of the emperor system still maintained its great authority over me. I was a sincere supporter of the emperor system; indeed, it was for the very purpose of supporting the emperor system that I wanted to become a historian!

The point on which I differed somewhat from others was that thanks to being an early bloomer, I read Minobe Tatsukichi's books on constitutional law at just about the same time. When I entered middle school, my second oldest brother was studying at Tokyo University of Commerce. Minobe was on the faculty of Tokyo Imperial University, but concurrently he was also a professor at Tokyo University of Commerce and taught the course there on constitutional law. My brother took Minobe's course and used as a text his *Essentials of Constitutional Law.* I read this *Essentials of Constitutional Law* that my brother was using, and I was deeply attracted, less by its intellectual content than by its brilliant logic, which almost resembled proofs in geometry. From that time to the present, for several decades, this book has been one of my favorites. At first, I borrowed my brother's copy; not until I was in

---

4. Tsuda Sōkichi (1873–1961): cultural historian.

high school did I buy my own copy of *Essentials of Constitutional Law* at a used bookstore. Even today a copy sits on my bookshelf, and on the back cover, in my own hand, is the date of purchase: May 1, 1932. That speaks of how great an influence this book had on me.

At the time I was captivated by the clarity of Minobe's logic. The influence didn't necessarily extend to intellectual content— his concepts of the state as legal person or of the emperor as organ of the state—but there can be no doubt that I accepted Minobe's constitutionalism without resistance. So even though I was true to the emperor system, something in my psychological makeup applied the brakes early and kept me from falling into a belief in fanatical emperor-system ideology. It was wholly a matter of chance, but coming into contact with Minobe's writing as early as year one in middle school has been a lifelong blessing.

Still, I cannot say that Minobe's influence on me has been completely a plus. Minobe argued explicitly that from the point of legal theory, the emperor was an organ of the state and that there were limits to the emperor's prerogative; but on the other hand, he recognized the existence of the concept of national polity as an ethical and historical reality. Indeed, by locking the concept of national polity out of the world of legal theory, he removed a way to protect the constitutionalism of the emperor-organ theory. As a legal scholar, Minobe was a decided proponent of constitutionalism—indeed, even of today's democratic attitude. But at the same time, he was also in part, emotionally, a true supporter of the ideology of the emperor system. I was bowled over and wound up in precisely the same position: on the one hand, a critical attitude toward fanatic emperor-system ideology was instilled in me; on the other, I was unable objectively to criticize the emperor system as a whole. That condition continued for several decades, and I was horribly late to open my eyes to the true essence of the emperor system. This was the minus side of Minobe's influence on me.

Whatever the case, in my middle-school years I completed the four-year course and moved on to higher school, lucky to have had something of an opportunity to study the limits of the orthodox morality, yet on the whole continuing to believe without doubt in the orthodox morality. My performance in my courses had been very spotty, and I had absolutely no confidence about the exams. So when it came time to select schools to apply to, rather than choosing the schools I really wanted to enter, I looked at the exams and chose the ones I thought would be easiest to get into. I had no choice. Today's high-schoolers may find themselves in the same situation. At that time private school S did not examine liberal arts candidates in mathematics, so I thought I was lucky that math wasn't involved and decided to apply there. The teacher in charge encouraged me to apply instead to First Higher (predecessor of today's Tokyo University Faculty of Liberal Arts). But I lacked the confidence that I belonged in the same room as the bright First Higher examinees, and I had some reservations—to be sure, they were no more than vague presentiments—about their ambitions to change the world. Moreover, I didn't think it was such a great honor to go to First Higher. So I had absolutely no desire to go to First Higher; I was irrational on the point. Higher school corresponded roughly with today's general education course at a university and was nothing else than the route to get into the university. If you could get into the specialized department of the university you wanted to attend, it didn't matter which higher school you went to. If I could only wriggle my way into some higher school . . . that's how I felt. And despite the teacher's encouragement, I declined to apply to First Higher and made private school S, easy to get into, my first choice. With the thought that if I got in, I'd go to a public higher school, I also sent in an application to Tokyo Higher School, a public institution. Fortunately, the two exams fell on different days.

Ironically, when I took the exam for S Higher, I skipped some problems and did a very poor job—in part out of uneasiness, the thought that I was in trouble if I didn't make it—and I failed utterly. But when it came to Tokyo Higher School, in which I had placed little stock, I got four out of five problems on the mathematics exam that was not my strong point, so it was possible to hope I might make it. I knew no greater joy than on the day the results were announced and I spotted my own number on the list of those who had made it pasted high on the outside wall of the school building. Thus in April 1931 I enrolled at Tokyo Higher School, bidding good-bye to the First Middle life that I had lived for five years (strictly speaking, four years and several months) and beginning my higher-school life.

4

A COPERNICAN REVOLUTION IN
MY INTELLECTUAL LIFE

In the sciences I was completely hopeless, so in higher school it was only natural that I choose Humanities, indeed Humanities Track I. (Track I meant English as first foreign language, Track II meant German, and Track III meant French.) I have studied English all my life and even gotten pretty good grades in it, but I must have no gift for languages. For all the studying I've done, I still can't use foreign languages as a practical tool. That's why I gave up on the study of foreign-language scholarship and chose my specialty from among fields for which I needed only Japanese. Thus, my deficiencies were not simply in the sciences; they manifested themselves in the humanities, too. As I realized step-by-step how unexpectedly broad my deficiencies were, a sense of hopelessness more and more hemmed me in. This, too, I'll touch on again later, but first I must speak of the fact that, after entering higher school, I experienced the most fundamental intellectual revolution of my life.

The spring of 1931, when I entered higher school, fell just before the Manchurian Incident, which broke out that September and belongs to the very tail end of Taishō democracy. Although, for reasons I've already mentioned, I didn't experience it personally, this was the height of the Shōwa terror. As social contradictions worsened, the accompanying tensions in the intellectual world grew more acute; Marxism took the intellectual world by storm. In the universities and the special higher schools, the student movement grew, and Tokyo Higher School apparently had many activists. Just before I arrived, several students were expelled for their ideas, and strikes to demand their readmission took place twice; I arrived in the very midst of that tension.

Photo 4.1 Classmates in higher school. Ienaga is second from right. Photo courtesy Ienaga Saburō.

Up until middle school, I had had no contact at all with such anti-establishment thinking; I hadn't the slightest doubt about the orthodox morality that had been infused into me at school. I'd need another whole volume to explain in detail just what that orthodox morality was, but if I were to summarize briefly the way of thinking I had been given, it would be something like the following. Japan was a country unique in the world in having had "one imperial family through all time," a "beautiful national character" with a proud tradition; because above all of the development of the great Japanese empire, the Japanese people should serve Japan at the sacrifice of all personal interests, including life itself. Another way of saying this is that ideas like socialism that disregarded this proud tradition and sought to destroy the "national polity" were anti-Japanese thoughts that no Japanese could tolerate.

Since reading *The Age of Yamato* and *Essentials of Constitutional Law*, I had made my own way of thinking that was to some extent rationalist, so I was not a true believer in the "concept of national polity" that in extreme forms could develop even into fanatical mysticism. But on the whole and fundamentally, I was sealed up inside the framework of this orthodox worldview. When, immediately after entering higher school, I came face-to-face with Marxism, this system that ran directly counter to the orthodox morality, it was a great shock.

Tokyo Higher School was a seven-year school, divided into two sections: the standard four-year middle school and the three-year higher school proper. Half the students came up through the standard school, and the other half entered from other middle schools. I entered in midstream, so I was not one of the insiders. There were many believers in Marxism, especially among those who had come up the inside route; even of those of us entering in the fifth year, a few had already received their Marxist baptism in middle school.

I don't understand fully the circumstances of the strike that took place before I arrived, but the demand that the expelled students be reinstated was rejected, so in the fall semester, the strike resumed. Even among us first-year students, there was fierce class debate as to whether to take part in this strike. I don't enjoy saying so, but as human beings most of the Marxists in my class were not very trustworthy, and I, of course, was a true believer in the concept of national polity. Immediately after coming face-to-face with Marxism, I experienced a strong reaction against it and, using my own naive logic, even argued with fellow students who believed in Marxism. In a sense it was an intellectual crisis for

The control under this [current] textbook certification system is extremely great compared with that in foreign countries, so improvement in the content of textbooks proceeds very slowly. Both logically and technically, the latent possibility exists to make Japanese textbooks into more understandable and bright textbooks different from today's; but the Ministry's central control blocks that from happening. . . .

Japan's textbook certification system is most problematic in that it presupposes distrust of teachers and distrust of pupils.
—Colleague's brief for lawsuit #3

Source: Shibata Yoshimatsu brief, quoted in Moritani Kimitoshi, "Kyōkasho no shippitsu to rekishi kenkyūsha," in *Rekishi no hōtei*, p. 180.

me: because of my antipathy to the Marxists, I really was in some danger of falling into the fascist camp. As I shall relate, I faced a similar crisis later, immediately after the war, but fortunately, both times I was able to avoid falling in either direction. In fact, that's been the story of my life.

This first crisis arose immediately after I entered higher school, but the Manchurian Incident that started in September gave it new force. The Manchurian Incident led the Japanese intellectual world to begin to turn to the right, and pressure against Marxists intensified. One after the other, Marxists apostasized from their Marxism, and as they did so, right-wing influence spread throughout the intellectual world. Just after the outbreak of the Manchurian Incident, a Marxist friend who sat immediately in front of me in class wrote "Down with imperialist wars!" in ink on a newspaper account of the incident, and during class he turned and slipped it to me. At the time I was so naive that I treated it as a joke.

Faced with the Manchurian Incident, we seemed to feel without knowing quite why that we had to do something. Having discussed the matter, our class agreed—by large majority over the strong opposition of those who believed in Marxism—to collect sympathy money for the families of the soldiers doing the fighting. One evening at Kagurazaka we actually solicited donations. Had these tendencies continued to hold, we might have been caught up completely in the militarist trend. We were lucky: I myself underwent a major intellectual change immediately thereafter, and most of the class, too, avoided going in the militarist direction. Still, there was a real danger that we would go that route.

Beginning about 1932, a great shifting of ground took place within me by slow degrees. To begin with, as I have already mentioned, with the passage of time my despair over my own talents became more urgent and more real, and I became engrossed in personal, internal—rather than political or social—thoughts. I have already noted that from infancy I have had to put up with many physical ailments and have suffered physical pain, and that since primary school I have been poor at science. From early on, these factors led me to fix my sights on the humanities. But once I entered the Faculty of Letters, I realized I was not a person who could simply take his pick of the humanities and gradually came to be acutely aware of how untalented I was. What profession would I, as a full-fledged member of society, ever be able to master? So I lost all confidence.

The last straw was that I rapidly lost interest in history, until then my chosen path. As I said a moment ago, my interest in history had been interest in narrative history. Confronted with heterodox ideas, with Marxism, I had to devote all my attention to a problem of theory—how to hold off this Marxist assault and carve out anew an intellectual position for myself. The result was that I lost interest in facts as opposed to theory and so could not sustain my interest in the study of history, in which facts are central.

I lost interest in history and focused all my attention on philosophy. Unable to accept Marxism with good grace, I did accept neo-Kantianism. Here my stodginess, my being always behind the times, put in a second appearance. After I became a specialist, I came to know that the age in which neo-Kantianism held sway was, of course, the 1910s and early 1920s; by the late 1920s that period in Japanese intellectual history was already over. Nevertheless, just as in middle school I had thrown myself into aping the new-style poetry of Tōson's Meiji era, so in higher school I discovered my escape in the neo-Kantianism of the age just past. What got me started was reading Tanabe Hajime's *Outline of the Sciences*, a book I happened to pick up in a second-hand bookstore.[1] It still sits on my bookshelf, and the date I bought it is inscribed: August 12, 1932. In the hot summer of 1932, sweat pouring off my brow, I tackled philosophy head-on for the first time.

Value judgments are absolutely necessary, to select from among countless events those that are necessary to include in a textbook, and these make possible different narratives reflecting differences in stances among individuals; so it is a very great miscalculation to use so very historian-like a term as "positivism" and say that all textbooks must be that or else.
—Criticizing a judge's logic, December 1997

Source: Ienaga, "Seishin no jiyu no tame ni tatakatta sanjūninen," *Rekishi chiri kyōiku* December 1997; in *Ienaga Saburō shuu*, vol. 14, p. 367.

---

1. Tanabe Hajime (1885–1962): philosopher, professor at Kyoto Imperial University.

When I reread this book now, I cannot pinpoint the source of the influence it exerted on me, what in it spoke to me; but after reading it, I experienced what was virtually a Copernican revolution. One after the other, I read the books of the German Southwestern school. (The Southwestern school was one branch of the neo-Kantians, represented by Windelband and Rickert;[2] it took a dualist stance, distinguishing sharply between *Sein* [is] and *Sollen* [ought], and emphasized *Sollen* as the source of norms; it was much in vogue among Japanese philosophers of the Taishō era.) I was fond of reading books like Rickert's *The Object of Knowledge*. It was not necessarily the case that I was influenced in specific ways by this one book, *The Object of Knowledge;* the whole Southwestern philosophy of *Sollen* was a new world for me, and for that very reason its influence was decisive. How fresh and alluring it was, this *Sollen* that was not *Sein,* this *Sollen* that indeed stood in opposition to *Sein.*

Indoctrinated into us from infancy through middle school, the "concept of national polity" based itself on the logic that the Japanese state had a polity unique among the nations of the world—one Imperial House since the dawn of creation. That is to say, the logical structure of the concept involved the justification of the present system in terms of past history; historical fact became the basis of *Sollen,* and norms of action were deduced from fact. The philosophy of the Southwestern school, which distinguished *Sein* sharply from *Sollen* and preached a clear break between the two, served to demolish this logical relation of *Sein* to *Sollen,* of history to practical action.

From the point of view of Marxism, of course, and even from my point of view today, the philosophy of the Southwestern German school is an extremely abstract system that leaves out the idea of historical development completely, and it cannot be called in any way politically progressive. But there's no rule that it has to be the historical and objective reality of a philosophy that influences people. The influence the Southwestern German school had on me was a case in point. Precisely because it sets *Sein* off against *Sollen* and construes fact and norm as separate, this philosophy cannot escape the criticism that it is abstract and one-

---

2. Wilhelm Windelband (1848–1915) and Heinrich Rickert (1863–1936): philosophers.

sided; yet it had the power to uproot the orthodox morality that for long years had ruled my mind. Through this philosophy of *Sollen* I was reborn. That is to say, through the medium of Southwestern philosophy I settled accounts with the national morality of Japanism and set out on a new life as a liberal. My intellectual life can be divided sharply into two parts, before and after, with 1932 as the boundary.

I say "liberal." Of course, looking back today, I see that what I experienced may have been no more than a revision of the nationalist creed to which I subscribed; still, neo-Kantianism rescued me from the danger of stumbling into fascism and gave me a non-Marxist intellectual position of my own. So 1932 is a very important year in my life. My ideas of the time are expressed in an essay, "On the Fundamental Problem of the Philosophy of the State," published in the eighteenth issue of Tokyo Higher School's *Magazine of the Liberal Arts*. This issue appeared in July 1933, and the essay exhibits traces of my agony in this transitional period; I tried to justify the state not by the naive nationalism I had supported until then but by my new liberalism. At its close, I listed as source materials Kant's *Critique of Pure Reason,* Rickert's *The Object of Knowledge,* Tanabe Hajime's *Outline of the Sciences,* and volume 1 of Minobe Tatsukichi's *Constitution of Japan,* and they explain the state of my thinking at that time.

In rough summary, this essay takes as its fundamental idea the neo-Kantian concept of the "pure state," and through a consideration of norms it seeks to ground the essence and appropriateness of the state in logic. In it, I cannot deny, there are still traces of the psychology of my long-standing nationalist era, and the workings of a will to justify the state one way or another are evident. But I wrote it after undergoing a fundamental change in thinking, so it does not seek simply to affirm the actual Japanese state out of hand; based on the new ideas, it reconstructs the state from a critical point of view and, having done that, tries to reevaluate its raison d'être. In part 4 of this essay is a section called "The Sanctioning of the Pure State," and in it I attempt to justify the state in a sense corresponding to the efficacy of laws (*die Geltung des Rechts*). The following passage shows for the first time the logical structure of the attitude toward the state that was mine thereafter, so I'll quote it here:

Practice aiming to create cultural values requires of course independence. When the state holds the governing power that
is accorded it in its supremacy, the doubt arises: doesn't the
state threaten this independence? However, the pure state is
a form of guarantee of life that accords with actual public
norms; forms of production and subjects of action are not the
same thing. Subjects of action are usually individuals, the
communal society linked to the individual, or the goal society;
the pure state does not produce art on its own. Independence
is required as a form of production only when subjects of action actually engage in the production of cultural values, so it
is not threatened by the essence of the pure state. But for that
reason the state is forbidden from becoming a producer of culture, and so the principle of externality—the second principle
of the theory of state policy—must arise; when this principle
is not respected, then the political exceeds its authority, as in
the suppression of freedom of religion. The policy that is
called liberalism also has its a priori basis in this principle of
externality.

I can't recall today what my immediate source was in writing
this passage; but in the book by Minobe Tatsukichi listed in the
bibliography of this essay, there is a passage that recognizes that
the modern state bears a broad responsibility for the active development of social culture, yet argues:

> It will not do to construe this to mean that the state can exer-
> cise any function at all, without limits. There must be fixed
> limits on the cultural duty of the state. As for scholarship, the
> arts, religion, and the like, they can be developed only through
> the free investigation of individuals. The function of the state
> in this regard is only the negative one of removing external
> obstacles that may hinder that free investigation; in a positive
> sense the function stops with the protection and encourage-
> ment of such development. To attempt by means of the power
> of the state to determine the direction of intellectual culture
> is to exceed the duty of the state.

Set this passage alongside my essay—it's likely I based myself on
it.

At the present time I have lodged a suit against the state,
claiming that textbook certification is illegal. As one of the points

in this suit, I interpret Article 10 of the Fundamental Law of Education to mean that the responsibilities of school administration are limited only to establishing the external conditions of education and do not intrude on educational content. I think it's worth pointing out that precisely the same formulation blossoms forth in this higher-school essay, my scholarly debut. In this essay I list "inclusivity" as a concept of the pure state, and on that point I argue that the pure state is unlimited in temporal and spatial terms, is essentially not unique, and is congruent more with a communal society than with a goal society. So when the concept of the pure state is made concrete in principles of state policy, the "principle of universality" must be established first, and in this universality there are two expansionist tendencies, external and internal. In the external dimension there is concentric development outward, from the small communal society such as hamlet or village, to the larger communal society such as the people, to the ultimate stage of universalism. At the same time, I clearly intend to affirm that even socialism is to be included in the concept of state philosophy in terms of internal expansion: "If you take democracy and the various social movements that have recently become important—for example, socialism, guild socialism, syndicalism—and trace them back a priori, each of these can be traced back to the latter concept [of internal expansion]." On this point this essay shows even more clearly that I had pretty much shed my prejudice against socialism; this prejudice, that socialism was "dangerous thought," had been indoctrinated into me from above by my public education in primary school, middle school, and, until that point, higher school. But at the time I knew nothing at all about class or bourgeois solidarity or about political mechanisms focusing on the opposition between independent bourgeois or class organizations, popular and autonomous, and state power, so I could not conceive of historical development based on horizontal mass organizations. In these respects I have to concede that seen from today, this essay has fatal flaws. Be that as it may, already in 1933 this essay pretty much sets forth—in youthful form, to be sure—the fundamental point of view that has been mine ever since, so it deserves a place in my personal intellectual history.

I have digressed; but in order to escape from the pressure of facts, I turned to the world of *Sollen* and thereby gained a new

> If, when Ienaga writes about the "human suffering" brought about by
> World War II, he were to change his wording and write of "pursuing and
> denouncing the following as crimes and the guilt of the Japanese govern-
> ment—deciding to go to war recklessly, persecuting the Japanese people,
> inviting ruin, and causing many deaths and injuries," that would be okay
> as moral stance or as essay on current events, but it is not historical judg-
> ment. Ienaga is supposed to be a historian; he should not run to this kind
> of argument anyone can make but should write about World War II more
> historically (scientifically). Because that's the special duty of a historian.
> —Ministry of Education bureaucrat, 1968
>
> Source: Murao Jirō, Yomigaeru Nihon no kokoro (Nihon kyōbunsha, 1968), pp.
> 58–59. Parentheses in original.

personal standpoint, and as a result of undergoing that change, I
lost interest completely in the academic discipline of history, in
which facts are primary. All this I have already described. Higher
school allowed three years in which to decide on a major field and
move on to the university. But after I entered that period of decision, my goal of many years' standing suddenly collapsed, leaving
me baffled. Given my interests of the time, it would have been
most natural for me to enter the philosophy department. But as I
have already noted, I had no confidence I could specialize in a
discipline in which foreign languages were central. In particular, I
had chosen Humanities I and not mastered German, so I couldn't
conceive of majoring in what interested me most—German philosophy. I didn't think that in real life I could make a living from
philosophy, so it stopped being an option for me.

Had I been in school merely with the aim of someday working for a top ministry or company and achieving the highest possible social status and salary, I probably wouldn't have had such
a rough time. But from the first that ordinary ambition to succeed
had not been my goal, so for me, the fundamental collapse of my
long-term goal was like losing my raison d'etre. I didn't know
what to do, and the anguish continued. Finally, the time to submit applications came. After vacillating and vacillating still more,
I made the Japanese history department of Tokyo Imperial University my first choice and sent off the application. It was a choice

born of desperation. On the one hand, I was clinging to force of habit—I had once liked history. On the other, Field A was not a possibility, nor was Field B, either, but maybe I could just manage Japanese history. So when I went to look at the announcement of exam results, there was absolutely none of the tension—a mixture of hope and anxiety—that I had experienced when I went to see the announcement of the results of the entrance exam for higher school. When I spotted my name among those accepted to my first choice, the department of Japanese history, I felt in fact slightly disappointed. Be that as it may, I became a student in the Japanese history department of the Faculty of Letters of Tokyo University. For better or for worse, my fate had been decided: from that day on I would specialize in Japanese history.

5

STUDENT LIFE AFTER THE EXTINCTION
OF THE STUDENT MOVEMENT

I had entered higher school as happy as if I were going to Heaven, but I entered Tokyo Imperial University still under a cloud of gloom. Anybody else would have envied me the Tōdai life [Tōdai is the short form for Tokyo University, *Tō*-kyō *Dai*-gaku], but I set out on it with ashen spirits. I had been absorbed entirely in issues of theory, and as I expected, the positivist spirit of the Japanese historians at Tōdai was unable to satisfy my mental hunger. I became more and more dejected, especially when told in my history courses that I could become a specialist only by mastering paleography. Not only was I no good at foreign languages, but old Japanese script was beyond my powers. I am so poor at deciphering old writing that even today I don't have the ability to read the correspondence of writers of the late nineteenth century, correspondence written in India ink in flowing script. I even remember fearing that if I had to master paleography to graduate with a degree in history, I might not make it. Nor was that all: at the reception for new students I heard that three of the students set to graduate that year in Japanese history had failed to make it. I thought I'd just entered a truly horrible place, and my dejection only grew worse.

It was not simply my despair about the academic side of things; intellectually, too, the Tōdai Japanese history faculty was an awful place. Here was Hiraizumi Kiyoshi, famous for being the most extreme Japanist. Things probably haven't changed much since then, and applicants for admission still don't check carefully ahead of time about the professors and assistant professors of the division to which they are applying. Even I knew that the Tōdai Japanese history faculty included Kuroita Katsumi, Tsuji Zennosuke, and Nakamura Kōya, but I truly wasn't aware of Hiraizumi's existence.[1] Then, when I actually enrolled, I found that Kuroita spent all his time on activities outside the university, that as head of the Historiographical Institute Tsuji hardly ever showed his face in a classroom, and that Nakamura, too, was assigned to the Historiographical Institute. Hiraizumi, assistant professor and student adviser, was in fact virtually the chief instructor with sole charge of the section. Course times, too, were arranged so that one had to take most classes with Hiraizumi.

Hiraizumi's text for the second-year seminar was *Azuma kagami*.[2] The basic techniques of historical reading that Hiraizumi taught us in this seminar on *Azuma kagami* were very useful thereafter, so in that sense I must be sincerely grateful for his instruction. But I was utterly unable to go along with his extreme Japanism.

For example, he taught that *kimi*, the familiar word for "you," was to be used in reference to the emperor only and for no other purpose. He didn't even use the term in its other reading, *kun*, to attach to the name of a student; he used *san* instead. When he spoke the names of Kitabatake Chikafusa or Kusunoki Masashige, he always appended *kō*, "lord"; when he said the names Yamazaki Ansai or Hirata Atsutane, he always added the honorific *sensei*, "master."[3] This was all a great surprise. The course that he said was about medieval Japanese history was really a history of the French Revolution; its main thrust seemed to be bitter criticism of the French Revolution for trampling so severely on the relation between lord and subject. I went to one lecture only, was shocked by it, and thereafter stopped going, so I can't be more precise, but it was a real scandal that this kind of thing went on in the guise of a course on Japanese history.

When I became a second-year student, Hiraizumi for some reason appointed me student member of the *Shigakkai* (Tōdai's history student association; it became a national scholarly organi-

---

1. Kuroita Katsumi (1874–1946), Tsuji Zennosuke (1877–1955), Hiraizumi Kiyoshi (1895–1984).

2. *Azuma kagami* (Mirror of the East): a history of the Kamakura shogunate compiled in the late thirteenth century.

3. Kitabatake Chikafusa (1293–1354): courtier, scholar, loyalist. Yamazaki Ansai (1619–1682): neo-Confucian scholar, founder of Suika Shinto. Hirata Atsutane (1776–1843): scholar of National Learning.

Photo 5.1   *Entering class in Japanese history, Tokyo Imperial University, 1934.*
In the front row, from the left, are Hiraizumi, Kuroita, Tsuji. Ienaga is in the center
of the fourth row from the front, the second student directly behind Kuroita.
Photo courtesy Ienaga Saburō.

zation, and in fact, thanks to the influence of Tōdai's history faculty, remains today the leading such association). The top leaders of the *Shigakkai* were professors from the history faculty, and under their direction young scholars who had just graduated—for the most part, teaching assistants—did the actual work; it was customary in addition to choose a student member from the second-year class. It frequently happened that I misread people and people misread me; Hiraizumi probably appointed me to be a member of the *Shigakkai* because he misread me. Whatever the case, I was assigned the task of helping with *Shigakkai* affairs. The director at that time, the one who supervised me, was Hirata Toshiharu (today a professor at the War College); he had graduated just as I arrived and was then an assistant. On occasion I had to write a book review for the journal's review column or write up an account of a study trip, and Hirata not only made arbitrary changes in what I wrote but even occasionally reversed my arguments. Amazed, I lodged a strong protest, but Hirata flatly rejected my protest. He claimed that what he had done was, of course, his prerogative as director; a journal had to be edited from a given point of view; a journal was not like a department store counter, with essays lined up indiscriminately. Even today I have not forgotten my resentment. And it taught me through personal experience that when such people gain the ascendancy in a society, full-blown fascism ensues. It was not simply that such conditions existed in the classroom; the whole atmosphere of Tōdai apparently had undergone a total change from what it had been before I arrived. In my higher-school years, indeed, already from my second year, it had become impossible to keep the student movement going; even had it been possible, I probably wouldn't have taken part. But when I entered the university, the student movement had already been suppressed completely. In 1933, the year before I arrived, the famous Takigawa Incident had occurred. Takigawa Yukitoki, who taught criminal law at Kyoto University, had been fired because of his theories. Out of solidarity with the Kyoto University students who organized in support of Takigawa, the Tōdai students as well organized a protest: in the middle of one of Minobe's classes students suddenly rose up, held Minobe captive in the classroom, and by main force held a student assembly. A police unit from the Motofuji Police Station was dispatched, surrounded the classroom, and arrested the students one by one as they came out. We knew that events like this had taken place, but after I enrolled in the university, there was not a single case of this kind of meeting or demonstration on campus. Nor did I ever see political handbills being distributed. I remember nothing more than being shocked by occasional inflammatory graffiti in the toilets: "Down with monarchy!" Such were the straits to which the student movement had been reduced.

During this period, too, the militarization of Japan, its turn to the right, deepened year by year. In 1935, when I was a second-year student, the dispute over the emperor-organ theory took place. Minobe Tatsukichi, the author of my beloved *Essentials of Constitutional Law,* came under violent attack by right-wing members of the Imperial Diet for advocating the theory that the emperor was an organ of the state. At first, the government argued on his behalf, but in the end it was forced to ban his major writings. Not only that, but pressured by the stubborn demands of the

> How many tens of millions—
> Japanese,
> Asians—
> dead due to
> state textbooks?
> —Poem sent in to Asahi poetry column
>
> Source: Poem contributed to *Asahi* poetry column by Mikihara Kazumasu; quoted in Ienaga, "32 Years of Fighting for Freedom of Thought," in *Ienaga Saburō shū*, vol. 14, p. 366 and in interview, "Of 32 Years of the Textbooks Suits and Japanese Culture," in *Ienaga Saburō shū*, vol. 14, p. 375.

right wing, the government was backed into a corner and had to decide whether to charge Minobe with a crime. Minobe escaped indictment by resigning his seat in the House of Peers reluctantly, but this incident was a great shock to me. I saved dozens of clippings from newspapers of the time about the issue—that shows how much my attention focused on this incident.

I had to write something about it, and there was no forum where as a student I could see my own writing in print, so I sent my reflections on the incident to *Daiichi*, the First Tokyo alumni journal, published in those days on an occasional basis. What I said was as follows:

So far as concerns the dispute over the emperor-organ theory, the writer has gone beyond indignation to disgust. I am by no means a supporter of Minobe's legal theory. Still, I must say this: it simply is intolerable that in the name of morality, the state suppresses someone's beliefs by brute force. To hand down an interpretation of the polity that is arbitrary and perverse and bigoted and then, when others differ from that interpretation even slightly, to seek to persecute them by calling them irreverent and treasonous: this is to turn the polity, revered by the entire nation, into a private thing and to give rein to private thoughts instead of respecting one's place. But if you listen to what they say, none of them promotes the theory of imperial sovereignty. They say it is wrong to discuss the polity in terms of rights and duties, but after all, what is sovereignty? Not only that, but their arguments are fraught with contradictions: they attack the concept of the state as legal person and consider the state simply as an abstract entity—a know-nothing stand that sinks to the level of the individualism they attack. They say that the emperor-organ theory is a direct import from Western scholarship, but so is the theory of sovereignty; open that concept up, and you find that its kernel is nothing other than absolutism in disguise. . . . That is because to regard Japan's polity as the same as the absolute monarchies of China and the West (some of them even go so far as to praise Qin Shi Huang Di's book-burning!) is to obstruct in the end the infinite development of our empire and to support the ruling class that mediates between imperial house and people. Conduct like this threatens the polity; it is an attitude that is most regrettable. When I think of our country's revered tradition, I feel deeply fortunate to have been born in Japan, but I am unable to be impressed in the slightest by the various adjectives they use in setting out their ideas. That is because everything they say is arid sophistry; it has not put down roots in the living and fervent sentiments of the people. Good-for-nothings who try to vilify persons of distinction only advertise their own worthlessness.

In the latter portion of this passage, there are some words singing the praises of the Japanese polity, but that is because at the time I really thought that way; I wasn't jumping on any bandwagon. Yet even I, standing where I did, couldn't stomach their persecution of Minobe.

Following the passage just quoted, I also criticized sharply the proposal to purge Western ideas, an argument that came into vogue about then. Here is my conclusion:

[T]he recent tendency to ultranationalism—the fact that its intellectual basis is mistaken notwithstanding—has encouraged the study of Japanese culture; for us who are specialists in that study, that is a welcome development. However, it is strange that from the same quarter come various insults to Japanese tradition. Picking flaws in *The Tale of Genji*, attempting to tamper with the posthumous works of Nichiren,[4] forbidding instruction in some Noh chants: these are insults. The works that have been handed down to us today as classics are

---

4. Nichiren (1222–1282): Buddhist leader, founder of Nichiren sect.

precious legacies from our ancestors, the crystallization of the Japanese spirit; to insult the classics is to slander our ancestors and destroy the spirit of Japan. Nor do these people have respect for Japanese history, either; perhaps we must be grateful, today being today, that the lewd portions of the *Kojiki* are not censored and that the extreme passages in the *Dainihonshi ronsan* are not suppressed.

With friends like these, who needs enemies? As I look at what is going on now in the public mind, this is what I see. Since the Manchurian Incident, the intellectual world of Japan as a whole has been in a frenzy. For the Japanese people today, the most important precept is summed up in the phrase: Watch out!

At the end stands the date, July 31, 1935, and the *Daiichi* that carried this essay was published on November 18 of that year. The editors who received this submission apparently were quite worried about publishing it; they changed the title of my draft from "Several Problems of Modern Thought" to "Several Modern Problems," and they changed the heading of the passage I quoted, "The Problem of the Emperor-Organ Theory," to "The Problem." The editors feared that this essay would cause the authorities to prosecute the journal, but for my part, I really had to get at least that much off my chest.

The same issue included a second essay, by a graduate of the third class, Shiromura Masujirō, entitled "The Clarification of the Body Politic." According to the biographical data the journal gave, the author was at that time a student in economics and politics at Waseda University. Dealing with the issue of the emperor-organ theory, he argued:

As subjects of the empire we should adhere to the theory that the emperor is sovereign. Still, that does not mean necessarily that we should accept all parts of the theories of Hozumi Yatsuka and Uesugi Shinkichi.[5] . . . The contempt for constitutionalism that is a weakness in the theory of both men goes against the gist of the Meiji Emperor's Five-Article Oath— "Seek broad debate and decide according to popular opinion"—and does not give adequate recognition to the existing

---

5. Hozumi Yatsuka (1860–1912) and Uesugi Shinkichi (1878–1929): conservative legal scholars.

structure of government. Along with the clarification of the polity, I wish to call for a clarification of the body politic.

The fact that an issue of a student magazine carried not one but two articles dealing with this incident testifies, I think, to how great a shock it was for us students.

In 1936 the February 26 Incident erupted. That year there were a number of heavy snows, and on the morning of February 26, too, it snowed heavily, so we attributed the absence of traffic in the city simply to the weather. But that afternoon we were stunned to learn that an army regiment had mutinied and was occupying the Prime Minister's Residence, the Army Ministry, and other buildings. After the war, documents were published that reported what took place inside the palace, and it became clear that the emperor was virtually alone in sticking from start to finish to a hard line against the rebel army. Strange to say, on the 27th we already knew about what was happening in the palace; I don't know how. I happened to be reading a book in the study hall and learned from a fellow student, now dead, Matsumoto Suteki, that the military leaders were meeting in the palace and debating countermeasures, that *"Tenchan"* was livid, and that they had beaten up General Mazaki. "Beaten up" was thrown in at the time to make the story more gripping; but that the emperor was livid was indeed actual fact, as we can see today from accurate records. It still puzzles me today that we should have known so quickly about so secret a matter. I didn't know what *Tenchan* [a familiar diminutive for the emperor, *Tennō*] meant, so I asked; even today I remember the answer clearly. One history of the postwar era written by a young historian after the war says that *Tenchan* was invented after the war, but that is a serious mistake. From personal experience I can attest that its use goes back at least to February 27, 1936. I have digressed; still, in those days events like this one followed one upon the other.

Because of these internal and external conditions—on the one hand, the lack of interest in these matters within the academic discipline of Japanese history; on the other, the oppression of the Hiraizumi ideology, which carried great weight among scholars of Japanese history—I spent my three years at the university full of bitterness. My mental state became one virtually of despair: if I can only write a thesis that will somehow pass muster

From the time my classmates and I entered the old higher school in 1932 until I began to think for myself, I accepted without question what was taught in the textbooks. Since I was in thrall to the prewar moral ortho-doxy, I had no critical consciousness where the war was concerned.

What in retrospect looks foolish is that I knew absolutely nothing about the real state of the war with China. There was absolutely no way the newspapers could print anything about atrocities or the Rape of Nanjing, of course, or Unit 731. I couldn't know that the war was aggression or that it was a dirty war. Still, having grown up in the era of "Taishō democracy," I understood well that England and the United States were mighty coun-tries. So on December 8, 1941, when I heard on the news that Japan had initiated war against these two countries, I knew instinctively that Japan was headed for disaster.

And even after the war, a good while passed before I read the report-ing of Edgar Snow and Agnes Smedley and understood Chinese popular resistance for the first time. I came to know, too, the essence of the China war. But of what's in my book on the Pacific War, half to three-quarters is stuff I picked up in my studies after the war. I studied the fifteen-year war just the way I studied the history of ancient and medieval times.

—*Interview, 1990*

Source: Interview with Sawachi Hisae, *Taidanshū*, pp. 94–95.

and get out of here as soon as possible. . . . There's no chance for someone so untalented as I to become a scholar. If I can only get a job that will put food on the table, then for the rest I'll spend my time reading the books I want to read. . . . While I was in this frame of mind, the annual study-excursion to the Kyoto area stimulated me to give Japanese history a serious try. It was then the custom in the first year to make an excursion to the Mito area; in the second year the excursion was to the Kyoto area. No doubt the excursion to Mito, homeland of the loyalist school of Mito Studies, was at the suggestion of Hiraizumi, and making the rounds of the sites connected with Mito Studies and Kitabatake Chikafusa formed the bulk of the schedule. I hadn't any desire to see such dumb places, so I didn't go.

But I was happy to go on the second-year excursion to west-ern Japan, to Kyoto and Nara. It was in December 1935, in the depth of winter, but I really did enjoy the excursion, seeing great works of ancient art day after day for a whole week. Looking back on my life, I think I never spent a happier week. On this trip, the Buddhist art of Yakushiji in Nara left the deepest impression on me. In particular, the majestic Yakushi trinity in the Golden Hall moved me deeply. Until then I hadn't known what to do for a thesis, but now the idea came to me to study the Jinshin Disturbance in order to clarify the historical origins of this magnificent Buddhist art. That is how I came to write a thesis on the intellectual history of the Asuka and Nara periods, focusing on the Jinshin Disturbance.

Twenty-five years later, on November 10, 1960, I set out for Yakushiji, and looking up at that beautiful pagoda, I recalled 1935 and surrendered to deep emotion. For so long, I had had no interest in Japanese history, but now, following the same path that led Watsuji Tetsurō[6] in his *Pilgrimage to Ancient Temples* to a new evaluation of ancient Japanese culture, I had been able to discover my own goal in Japanese history, a goal about which I cared deeply. What gave me my research theme was Shōtoku Taishi's statement, "In this world all is vanity; only the Buddha is true." These words drew me to this man of thought, Shōtoku Taishi. Shōtoku Taishi and the Jinshin Disturbance: with these as my two focuses, the theme of my thesis was set.

I had lost interest in facts in favor of philosophy and theory, but in order to graduate I had to write a history thesis. If I was to pique my own interest, I thought, the only way was to work in intellectual history, the field closest to philosophy. In fact, my main field down to the present has been intellectual history, and that is how it all came about. Consequently, when I first turned my attention to Buddhism, I restricted my attention solely to the doctrinal aspect, symbolized by the words of Shōtoku Taishi I've just quoted; I had virtually no interest in the cultural aspect. With the excursion to the Kansai, my interest broadened to include Buddhist culture. But before getting to that, I must go back in time once more and speak of the birth of my interest in Buddhism.

I have mentioned how, when I was a first-year student in middle school, *Essentials of Constitutional Law* was favorite reading, and from early on I had focused a lot of attention on the state.

---

6. Watsuji Tetsurō (1889–1960): philosopher; cultural historian.

Photo 5.2 The class excursion to Kyoto and Nara, 1936. At the ruins of Asuka Honyakushiji. Photo courtesy of Ienaga Saburō.

That I accepted the orthodox morality without resistance was not simply the result of having it poured into me through the pipe called education, with me entirely passive; it was rooted also in the fact that in my own mind I always placed the state foremost, the state that transcends individuals. I have already noted that in primary school, when Okano asked us why we were going to school, I was the only one to answer, "For the state." From childhood, my mind harbored a tendency toward nationalism. The early stages of my personal intellectual history began not with thoughts about internal—individual—issues but with thoughts about issues of society, the state. Marxism's impact on me just after I entered higher school caused me agitation and for a while took the form of a reaction against Marxism; to regain my footing, I underwent a major intellectual change. Afterward, despite my reaction against Marxism emotionally, Marxism left an ineradicable effect on my thinking. I read only a few of the Marxist classics at that time, and my level of understanding was not high, but they taught me a new way of seeing many things that had been blind spots for me. These included the historical and social meaning of class, the concept of production forces and relations of production as fundamental forces that determine history, and the like. In particular, as I've already noted, I hadn't experienced life at its depths, but in infancy I had tasted the bitterness of poverty, so in fact the ground was prepared for me to respond positively to the demand for the liberation of the unpropertied classes. Since then, I have neither endorsed Marxism nor separated myself from it. In fact, I did study Marxism seriously, but I never became a "Marxist." I have not been stingy with high praise for Marxism as one of the outstanding philosophies, sciences of society, and practical theories that mankind has produced, and I stand in decided opposition to the anticommunists. But for me, Marxism is neither more nor less than one of the supreme and varied legacies of human thought, like Buddhism, Christianity, and the others.

I may be thought self-important to compare myself to distinguished predecessors, but still I draw this analogy. In his autobiographical *Delusions,* Mori Ōgai[7] says: "I stood at a crossroads, and time and again I doffed my cap. Among the ancients, among the

7. Mori Ōgai (1862–1922): medical doctor; novelist, critic.

people of today, there were many deserving of my respect. I doffed my cap, but I didn't leave the crossroads to follow any of them." In that spirit I have learned much from great ideas old and new, East and West, but to this day I have been unable to commit myself completely to any of them. I think one can make distinctions among ideas that contain much truth, ideas that involve some truth and some falsehood, and ideas that are utterly unacceptable. But I simply cannot believe that there is an idea that is omnicompetent, that supplies a complete answer to every last problem, that makes all other ideas unnecessary, that is like Monkey's staff of truth in *Journey to the West*[8] or the magic lamp in *The Arabian Nights*. For me, it is unthinkable that an idea exists that is like the trump in the game of Sugoroku—get it, and all earlier ideas become unnecessary, and there is no longer a need for any new ideas. I have always wanted to view the entire development of all human ideas as broadly as possible and to foster the development of my own ideas by studying as many truthful ideas as I could. Since 1932 my attitude has seen its ups and downs and some changes, but its basic outlines have held constant. Still, within that framework, waves have done their buffeting since then, perhaps more in my case than in the case of other people.

After my intellectual turning point of 1932, I focused my attention at first solely on the personal/internal dimension. This is

Today is the age of propaganda. Propaganda is carried out tirelessly that takes up issues on which it is easy to appeal to public opinion and that aims ultimately at revolution. The university unrest, the Narita airport struggle, and so on—the issues are beyond counting, and the recent pollution problem is no exception. The textbook trials emerge out of this background.
    —President of Ienaga's university, 1970, and Ienaga's antagonist in both the university struggle and the textbook trials

Source: Miwa Tomio, in Miwa, ed., *Kyōkasho saiban: ronsō to hihan* (Teikoku chigō gyōsei gakkai, 1970), p. i. For Miwa's role in Ienaga's struggles at Tokyo University of Education and against the Ministry of Education, see chapter 10.

---

8. Wu Cheng'en's *Xiyouji* (sixteenth century).

why: as I have said repeatedly, because of my own abilities and physical afflictions I have had to put up with suffering, and so through the lens, first of all, of my own experience I have had to think seriously about the problem of human limitations. In this period I happened to read Shinran's[9] *Tannishō*. His words made a major impression on me:

> The Primal Vow was established out of deep compassion for us who, due to the abundance of blind passion, cannot be freed from the bondage of birth-and-death through any religious practice. Since its basic intention is to effect the enlightenment of evil people, the evil person who entrusts himself to Other Power is truly the one who attains birth into the Pure Land. Thus, even the good person attains birth; how much more so the evil person!

Again:

> I asked, "Although I say the *nembutsu,* I rarely experience joyful happiness, nor do I have the desire to go immediately to the Pure Land. What should be done about this?" Then he responded, "I, Shinran, have been having the same question also, and now you, Yui'en, have the same thought."
>
> "When I consider the matter carefully, it is without doubt that my birth into the Pure Land is settled for the very reason that I do not rejoice at that which should have me bursting with joy. It is the working of blind passion that suppresses the heart that would rejoice and prevents its fullest expression. All this the Buddha knew already and called us foolish beings filled with blind passion; thus, when we realize that the compassionate Vow of Other Power is for beings like ourselves, the Vow becomes even more reliable and dependable."

I had entered the world of philosophy via the neo-Kantians and for a while had thought that Western philosophy had produced the only theoretical worldviews there were. But to learn that such superb ideas existed in the Japanese intellectual world, too, opened a new prospect for me.

I even took another look at Buddhism, which until then I had

---

9. Shinran (1173–1262): founder of Jōdo shin sect of Japanese Buddhism.

known only ceremonially, from funeral services. And as I reexamined Buddhism, my eyes were opened also to Christianity. In particular, many of the words of Paul in the Book of Romans went straight to my heart. "Since all have sinned and fall short of the glory of God, they are justified by his grace as a gift, through the redemption which is in Christ Jesus;" "For we hold that a man is justified by faith apart from works of law;" "Law came in, to increase the trespass; but where sin increased, grace abounded all the more." How well these words matched the teachings of Shinran! Through Shinran and the Bible I took up the problem of religion in a serious way. That is one reason I was so moved by Shōtoku's "In this world all is vanity; only the Buddha is true." I understood that statement in terms of my own experience of the limits of my body and the limits of my talents; seeing in my afflictions symbols of the fundamental sin of mankind, I also became aware as one human being of the depth of my own sin. In the dualism of *Sollen* and *Sein,* one can go only so far as the stage of relative negation, of the critique of *Sein* via *Sollen,* but now I reached the point of comprehending a logic of absolute negation based on the dualism of this world and the other world. That was a structure of existence far more fundamental than the opposition of *Sein* and *Sollen.*

As a student of history, I had chosen to specialize in intellectual history and focus on the problem of "salvation" via the absolute negation of the ego, so it was entirely natural that the research topic in intellectual history on which I settled focused on religious thought. My work appeared in 1938 as a series of articles in the journal *Rekishigaku kenkyū* and then in 1940 as a book entitled *The Development of the Logic of Negation in Japanese Intellectual History;* it is dear to me not only because it shows in straightforward fashion my scholarly problem-consciousness at that time but also because it became the prototype of my methodology of intellectual history. Be that as it may, I gradually became engrossed in religious issues; little by little I lost the strong interest I had once had in issues of state and society. This condition continued for several more years after I graduated from the university. In those years the Japanese intellectual world turned ever right, to the extreme that if you were not a Japanist, you were considered a traitor. But because I happened to turn away from issues of state and society, I was able to avoid being swept up in that movement. That I could avoid being swept up was due to the conditions I have described, not to any exceptional strength of intellectual conviction. It is not something to be proud of, but as I have said, I was stodgy, always following anachronistic ideas remote from the vanguard. So it is perhaps an irony of fate that in an age in which the whole nation turned right, I avoided jumping aboard the Japanist bandwagon.

6

MY LIFE AS A SCHOLAR, BEGUN IN THE ERA OF THE "DARK VALLEY"

Professors of Japanese history at Tōdai gave me much that I am grateful for, and Tsuji and Sakamoto[1] in particular showed me many kindnesses that extended long after graduation and even to personal matters. Still, insofar as scholarship and ideas are concerned, I was loyal disciple to none of them. In scholarly and intellectual terms I was influenced most not by the professors with whom I worked closely but by others. For example, the greatest influence of all came from Tsuda Sōkichi's critique of the *Kojiki* and *Nihongi* and his studies in intellectual history.[2] I can't write or say enough in particular about the impact of his four-volume work *An Inquiry into the Japanese Mind as Mirrored in Literature;* written during the Taishō era, it is a book I read after graduating. The world looked very different after I read this work: that's how great its impact was. Again, I was influenced greatly by the writings on the founding of ancient temples of Fukuyama Toshio, who worked in relative obscurity yet published excellent essays in rapid succession. I had had no interest in fields like historical investigation that were the furthest removed from philosophy, but Fukuyama's many essays taught me how fresh and wonderful even historical investigation can be in the hands of a highly skilled practitioner.

Yet even though at heart I had negative feelings toward it, the positivism of Tōdai's Japanese history faculty was what influenced me decisively and ineradicably, and this was not simply Fukuyama's doing. As I have already mentioned, from the time I arrived

---

1. Sakamoto Tarō (1901–1987): historian.
2. Tsuda Sōkichi (1873–1961): cultural historian.

I had been assailed by sharp fears that anyone who entered by mistake, as I had, would have a very difficult time graduating. So when it came time to write my thesis, I gave my all to produce a thesis that could pass muster somehow, an eminently positivist thesis supported by elaborate and precise evidence. As a result, positivism soon became my second nature, and even after I graduated, with flunking out no longer a worry, when I wrote books and articles, that second nature governed me without my knowing it. And so I came to write books I could not have dreamed of in my young-philosopher days—*Studies in the Theory of Kingship of Shōtoku Taishi* and *Chronology of Early Yamato-e.* I'm not a very loyal alumnus, but that's how strong an imprint on my scholarship the positivism of the Tōdai Japanese history faculty left. On the other hand, my interests from those young-philosopher days gave me a strongly subjective problem-consciousness, and that problem-consciousness gave rise to certain approaches to intellectual history. These approaches have joined with positivism in strange ways to give my scholarship the appearance of a methodological split, a dualism in my writing that may never find resolution. That is a story for later.

To return to my narrative: I wasn't even confident my thesis was good enough to pass, but to my surprise it received high praise from Tsuji in particular, and I was invited to join the Historiographical Institute.[3] Receiving praise from Tsuji, positivist par excellence, was unexpected enough, but being encouraged to stay on with the Historiographical Institute was not simply unexpected—it was downright bewildering. The Historiographical Institute was entrusted with the editing of *The Historical Materials of Japan* and *The Documents of Japan,* and there was absolutely no way I should work there; among other things, I was utterly unable to read old manuscripts and documents freely. Moreover, given my makeup, it was probably the most unlikely place in the world for me to work. But getting a job at the Historiographical Institute was considered a high honor for graduates in Japanese history. In fact, the people who had preceded me there were all outstanding men, so I simply couldn't get up on my high horse and reject the excessive, unmerited encouragement of Tsuji. And

---

3. Historiographical Institute (1869–present): affiliated with Tokyo University, the most important history research institute for Japanese history.

if I were to turn the job down, I hadn't a clue how else to make a living. I joined the Historiographical Institute in precisely the same dubious frame of mind I was in when I began Japanese history reluctantly at Tōdai.

During the five calendar years I worked at the Historiographical Institute, I was able to spend my time in ways that were of great benefit to my scholarly life. In that sense I am still most grateful for Tsuji's kind words in praising me too highly, and I wish to note my heartfelt thanks as well for the friendliness of my seniors and colleagues then at the Historiographical Institute. Though I was an absolutely incompetent newcomer, they received me warmly. I was assigned to the section that was compiling *The Historical Materials of Japan,* and under the direction of Nishioka Toranosuke,[4] I was put to work editing manuscripts.

In those days if you checked in by 9:30 A.M., you weren't considered late to work, and if I'm not mistaken, the office closed at 4:30. I decided always to get to work by 8:30 and to do my own research until 9:30, when everyone else showed up. And I didn't leave the office at 4:30 but stayed and worked on my own research until about 5:30. As for the editing, my quota for the month was pretty much set, and once I completed that, I was relatively free to do whatever I wanted. I finished my assignment in the shortest possible time and then could use all the rest of the time for my own research. What is more, the Historiographical Institute, which had a line-up of specialists on every age from the Heian down to early Tokugawa, included experts on virtually every aspect of Japanese history. If I had a question about something, I could always find someone who knew the answer. From the perspective of the Historiographical Institute, I was a most useless employee—that's beyond doubt; yet thanks to the people there, I was able to learn a lot. Still, to tell the truth, it was when I was a third-year student at the university, writing my thesis, that I threw myself most completely into my studies. By the end of my second year I had taken virtually all the courses, so for a full academic year, my third, I spent all my time on my thesis. Then, for some years after graduating, I lived off the capital I had accumulated in that one year.

While I was working at the Historiographical Institute, I

---

4. Nishioka Toranosuke (1895–1970): historian.

completed, one after the other, the essays I published in 1942 as
Studies in Ancient Buddhist Intellectual History. The essays gathered in
part 1, "Studies of Shōtoku Taishi," and part 2, "Studies in Nara
Buddhism," were little more than expansions of sections of my
thesis—my thesis peddled piecemeal. Only part 3, "Studies in
Heian Buddhism," was written after I had joined the Historiographical Institute, based on knowledge I gained in working on
the compilation of the second *Historical Materials of Japan*.

I began publishing the year I graduated, and I proceeded to
publish journal essays, one on the heels of the last. I was unable
to frame a huge topic, settle down, and come to grips with it over
the long term in lengthy works. Instead, it became my habit to go
to print piecemeal with the results of my research, and that has
been my scholarly habit now for thirty years. I settled consciously
on this procedure for several reasons. First, I had no confidence
that I, who was sickly, would live long. Second, the war was getting fierce—the war with China gradually becoming war with England and America, so that even if I didn't die of disease, I
couldn't tell when I might lose my life in the war. Third, I felt
strongly that if I put whatever I had completed into print at the
earliest possible opportunity, then it might be said that even my
humble life was not completely meaningless. So from the launch-
ing of my scholarly life, I kept my eye always fixed on death; I
wanted to leave behind work in print for every single day I was
alive, even if that work hadn't ripened fully. My awareness of the
transient nature of life determined my attitude toward my scholarly life. It was the same sense as in the famous song: "The cherry
blossoms that count on tomorrow / get scattered by tonight's
storm." As I worked away editing the Heian materials, part of my
job was to read Heian-era documents, and gradually the scope of
my studies extended to later periods. Meanwhile, among the documents of the Heian era, I discovered almost by chance all kinds
of documents about *Yamato-e*, medieval Japanese paintings, and I
began to study these paintings as a sideline. The research notes
that I had strung together as foundation for that study happened
to catch the eye of Yashiro Yukio, then the chief of the art history
section,[5] and I was fortunate enough to publish them in 1942 as
Chronology of Early Yamato-e. The trip to the Kansai in the winter of

5. Yashiro Yukio (1890–1975): art historian.

1935 had opened my eyes to the world not simply of intellectual history but of cultural history, and after graduation, as a sideline to the intellectual history of Buddhism, I extended my reach to this realm of cultural history.

Chronology of Early Yamato-e was the documents, and *History of Early Yamato-e* was the research; these companion studies of *Yamato-e* arose as a by-product of the intellectual history of Buddhism in the Heian period to which I set my hand after joining the Historiographical Institute. Further, during the war I completed the draft of the two-volume *Studies in the Kingship Theory of Shōtoku Taishi* that Sanseidō published after the war; toward the end of the war I completed drafts as well of *Studies in Medieval Buddhist History* and *On the Reception of Foreign Culture into Japan.*

Thus, the themes of my research changed continually. As I will relate later, after being appointed to Niigata Higher School, I leaped in one bound from the late middle ages to modern intellectual history, and after the war I suddenly switched horses and became a modern historian. By no means do I think this sort of approach to research is a sound one, nor would I advise anyone to imitate it; it was little more than what was forced upon me by my lack of talent and stamina. I was not blessed with the physical constitution to frame a vast topic, stick to it, and investigate it to its depths; as untalented as I was, in pursuing a given topic, I immediately encountered obstacles and couldn't set for myself the longer-term goal of investigating issues in greater depth. So when I was deadlocked, my only escape was to switch topics. Moreover, there was another significant factor: the custom I've described of publishing piecemeal, one essay after another, led naturally to a tendency to avoid taking on grand topics. Even granting that people have different ways of operating, each according to his gifts, my approach to research was an anomaly that cannot be recommended for others; still, it was all I could manage. But this way of doing things was not necessarily a total loss. It had, I think, an unexpected gain: even after I got quite old, each time I shifted to a new topic, I could study it with a spirit as fresh as that of a novice researcher just embarking on a scholarly career.

I graduated in March 1937, shortly before the outbreak of the Marco Polo Bridge incident that became the beginning of all-out war between Japan and China. That conjunction echoed the earlier one, that I had entered higher school in April 1931, just before the outbreak of the Manchurian Incident. At the time students could defer their induction into the armed forces, and I had put off taking my physical. But I graduated in 1937, and so I finally had to take it. Those who had deferred induction were left until last, and on July 31, at the ward offices of Setagaya-ku, I took my physical. A receptionist from the ward offices called out our names, last names only with no honorifics, giving us right at the start a foretaste of military impersonality. I also witnessed a scene in which M., a classmate of mine from higher school who happened to take his physical at the same time as I, was bawled out for not replying immediately to the questions of the N.C.O. measuring his height. At the end, we stood in front of the officer to hear the announcement of our classification, and I had to repeat back to him, "Ienaga Saburō: 4-F." I repeated "Ienaga Saburō: 4-F" as happy as if I were entering paradise. Joy welled up inside me, for this classification severed all connection with the military for the rest of my life, but I fought to hide my reaction. To be sure, afterward even the 4-F people were called up, so this joy was premature. . . . But the main thing was that I was able now to concentrate on my research without fear of military service. Most of my classmates were classified 1-A and conscripted.

Among the classmates lounging in the library while I was writing my thesis, one of the constant topics was how to avoid military service. The weaklings like me who could predict that they would be classified no higher than 4-F listened almost as bystanders to the anguish of friends who had no hope of avoiding 1-A. Once one of us egged them on: "Is being conscripted as horrible as all that?" They responded with real anger: "You don't have to worry. Try putting yourselves in our shoes." Anyone sentenced to a punishment of more than six years was exempted from military service, and I remember jokes about that: Wasn't penal servitude better than military service? And if it's going to be penal servitude anyway, why not be convicted of rape? That's how important the issue of military service was for our generation. Perhaps all of us had the devil's own luck, for not one of my classmates at Tōdai died in the war, but some were wounded on the China front and even today sometimes feel their injuries. It doesn't matter whether you saw action; in the minds and bodies of our generation, the war left scars that will never fade. Later, even the 4-F people were called up, and I, too, tasted—if only in greatly attenuated form—the reality of the Imperial Army: being shouted at by the leader from the reservist organization at periodic muster, being bawled out at roll-call by the drill sergeant. But I was never summoned to active duty, and the day of defeat dawned without my ever having been in the military. Thinking back now, I was extraordinarily fortunate to get by without experiencing life in police detention cells or in the army, yet that meant I missed the opportunity to know the real state of "the Great Japanese Empire." What I mean is that the detention cells and the army, where naked force ruled in a situation outside the law, symbolized best "the Great Japanese Empire." Without experiencing them, one might not be able to understand the essence of "the Great Japanese Empire."

I was classified 4-F. But as the war got fiercer, those subject to conscription were called to periodic musters, and to prepare for those, we had to take part in Reservists' Association training. With illness as my excuse, I sought to avoid this training as much as I could, but even I couldn't get by without ever showing my face. The following incident took place while I was employed at Niigata Higher School, on the parade ground of the Niigata branch of the Reservists' Association. It was the night before muster, and drill went on until about 10:30. One person couldn't take it any longer. He went to the section chief and asked: "Tomorrow's muster is a formal affair. I want to take a bath and be clean for muster, so please can't we call it quits for tonight?" It was really a brave speech. But there was one scatterbrained fellow, and he raised his voice: "Right on!" Immediately, the top brass of the branch association shouted, "This is the army! What's this 'Right on' stuff? Fall out!" They dragged the fellow out and punched and kicked him for a long time. It was so brutal that finally the branch chief shouted, "Enough!" I felt I was getting a peek at one remove into life in an army unit. After the war I saw Ishikawa Tatsuzō's movie *Reeds That Blow in the Wind*. Having been conscripted into the army, the hero cannot behave with the requisite discretion, and, kicked by an N.C.O., he becomes sick and finally dies. Had I been conscripted, that probably would have been my fate. As I watched this movie, I reflected once more on my good fortune.

The most painful thing about student life was that we were virtually stripped of academic freedom and the freedom of expression. For me, specializing in Japanese history where the scholarly and intellectual restraints were tightest, this was a serious problem. In one passage of my thesis I had given a historiographical gloss for the famous oracular text that reads "coeval with Heaven and earth." It was probably somewhat risky to do this in a thesis that had to withstand the examination of the entire faculty, including Hiraizumi. But perhaps because Tsuji was still in charge at the time, no problems arose, at least insofar as the thesis was concerned. Puffed up with success, I decided after graduation to try to publish this section of my thesis as an essay. At the time my seniors at the Historiographical Institute published a journal called *Rekishi chiri,* and I submitted an article entitled, "On the Establishment of the Oracle, 'Coeval with Heaven and Earth.'" From what happened afterward, I imagine that the editors must have reacted with shock on seeing this title; but it got past the editorial board in that form, was sent off to the printers, and got as far as galley proofs. At this stage, the editors succumbed to the fear that if they published it as it stood, the entire issue of the journal might be censored, and they came to me first with a request to change the title. The ostensible reason was that the title stuck out too much. I could hardly not go along with so minor a change, so I changed the title to "On the Establishment of the Oracular Text in the *Nihongi,* Book I" and thought that would do it. But at that point the editors got more and more worried and, as a result of consultations with our most senior colleagues, came to me with the request that I withdraw the essay. I faced my first test: to fight for academic freedom or to compromise. Only Nishioka, the head of my section, said to go ahead and publish it even if that meant incurring the wrath of the censors; the editors younger than Nishioka all thought the essay shouldn't be published. One senior colleague turned to me and said, "I understand you've written an irreverent essay." Another said, "There are plenty of other topics to study." I felt I was seeing into the very heart of the scholarship of the historians of the Historiographical Institute. At the time I was a completely unknown young man, so despite what might have been the case with the work of a great scholar, I didn't think an essay I wrote would be a problem; even if some sanction were imposed, I resolved inwardly to put up with it. But because of the way the system worked, the responsibility fell not only on the author but also on those involved in the publication. So even though I was for going ahead, I thought I had to keep the complications from extending to my elders. I swallowed my tears and withdrew the essay. In the end, this manuscript, my first scholarly essay to be set in print, died and was buried at the galley-proof stage, and until the defeat I had no choice but to keep it under lock and key. This was what I experienced in my initial outing as an academic researcher. It is, I think, one of the experiences that shape my conduct today. At the time my consciousness had not been raised, and I didn't feel any great responsibility to uphold academic freedom, but in my initial outing as a scholar I experienced firsthand the severity of the restrictions on academic freedom and freedom of expression under the Meiji Constitution.

I was employed at the Historiographical Institute until May 1941. There I could work on my own research to my heart's content, but I never thought of it as a place to stay long. In May 1941 my classmate S. received an invitation to transfer to Niigata Higher School. But family considerations forced him to refuse,

---

My insistence on freedom of expression, too, has this pre-history [of the censorship of his very first essay]. I hope people realize that I didn't speak out suddenly simply because I got manhandled in the certification process. [His interviewer speaks of listening to Ienaga lecture in 1952 on resistance among commoners toward samurai and comments that that lecture was not unrelated, either.] Hmm. In those days right after the war, social concerns had fallen to their lowest ebb. I've always benefited from instruction by negative example. The year I entered higher school was the year the Manchurian Incident began, and there was support for the war. When I was at Tōdai in Japanese history, Professor Hiraizumi provided the negative example. Just after the defeat, I reacted against a democracy that seemed as easy as one, two, three; I even risked turning right-wing. While I taught at Tokyo University of Education, the university's undemocratic administration provided the negative example I learned from. As the movement to revise the constitution gained strength, I took part . . . in the struggle to support the constitution. These experiences accumulated, and they did all connect to the textbook suits.

—Interview, 1994

Source: Interview with Yanagida Setsuko, in *Taidanshū*, pp. 163–164.

and the offer then came to me. I had grown up only on the side of Japan facing out onto the Pacific Ocean, and the very thought of living in Niigata gave me shivers. But the chance, barely five years after graduating, to become a professor in a higher school was one in a thousand, and I was not likely to have another opportunity to escape from the Historiographical Institute. So half in desperation I accepted this offer and moved to Niigata. Professor at a higher school: this was a post with real allure, and in my heart of hearts I had longed for such a post since student days. But try as I might, I couldn't work up any enthusiasm about going to the snowbound world of Niigata. May 1941 was shortly before war with the United States broke out. Rationing had already begun, and if you didn't have access to the black market or connections, it was difficult to get food and the other necessities of daily life. So going off to a place where I had absolutely no connections, I had to live a very constrained life.

The Japan that faces out onto the Pacific has autumn days when the weather is fine, but not Niigata. Once autumn comes, Niigata doesn't get many days of sunshine, and around November the rains begin to fall. Unable to afford a second pair of boots even after my first pair got soaked, I had to go to work in waterlogged boots. After New Year's the snow piles up, becoming the "snow that stays;" it freezes into ice and piles up three feet high. If you forget and walk the streets in normal footwear, you're sure to slip and hurt yourself. It's a region with dreadful weather: on blizzard days you can't control an umbrella, and men go about wearing ski caps. In that gloomy Niigata, one single majestic scene remains even today branded on my retinas: a winter day, sky perfectly clear as was only occasionally the case, the mountains we could see off to the south festooned with snow. It made me wonder whether Vienna, too, didn't look like this. Niigata prides itself on just such views.

Here I gave my first lectures. For a dozen years or so I had sat in classrooms facing the front; now for the first time I became one of those who stood with their backs to the blackboard. At the time higher-school students still had the same disposition they had in my student days, and as I stood at the front, indecisive, they immediately heckled me. Still, I liked that because it awoke in me memories of my own higher-school days. But in the short time— three calendar years—I taught there, things changed rapidly. Day

Photo 6.1 Ienaga in Niigata classroom. Date uncertain. Photo courtesy Ienaga Saburō.

by day the controls on education—both primary and secondary—were tightened, and the wild student life I had known as a higher-school student suddenly disappeared completely. Military training was intensified, and it came time for faculty, too, to take part in inspection; I remember wrapping on gaiters and strapping on a sword as captain of a patriotic unit and marching along with the students. The principal was a very weak person. When he received the request from the military that during inspections the faculty also march as captains of units, he put that request before the faculty. Normally, it was the custom to hand down decisions only after listening carefully in a faculty meeting to the opinion of each faculty member. Virtually the entire faculty was opposed, but despite that fact the principal said, "You don't like it, I know, but please put up with it," and in the end, on his order, the change was carried out. At the time one physical education teacher commented ingratiatingly, "Even women are training for the fire brigades. What's the big deal about higher-school faculty being unit chiefs in the patriotic corps?" It was a pleasure when a senior teacher, normally a firm conservative, responded, "We are professionals." This firsthand experience impressed upon me that every age has its toadies.

Higher-school education collapsed; worse still, primary school and middle-school education collapsed, too. To be sure, the students I had in my first year had received the same nationalistic education I had received or more of it, so they behaved boisterously with the privilege still accorded by force of habit to the student elite. Yet at the decisive moment, they didn't have what it took to stand up and be counted. On December 8, 1941, the day war with the United States began, when the radio brought the news of the opening of hostilities, I knew that Japan finally had set out on the road to destruction, and I felt absolute frustration. There was no radio in my house, so I went to school not knowing the early-morning news of the opening of hostilities. Learning from a colleague in the faculty lounge that war had begun, I was stunned. Still, in a philosophical mood I tried to begin the day's teaching. I started to pick up where the last lecture had left off, without mentioning the war news at all, but a student excited by the news of "great success" in the attack on Pearl Harbor said, "Teacher, why aren't you excited?" I listened sadly to the stu-

When I began teaching the survey of Japanese history at Niigata, I had studied only ancient history, and I still had lingering traces of my youthful interest in philosophy, so I did a kind of historical/philosophical outline of history.

In regard to the beginning of Japanese history, I said, "The tales of the age of the gods are beliefs of the people in ancient times." It wasn't "the people"; it was the "officials of the court"; but I could only use the going term of the time, "the people." And "beliefs"—that was my way of intimating that this wasn't historical fact. At that time this was my greatest act of resistance. In the classroom, not like today, there were right-wing students, too, and it was almost as if I were being made to trample on a Christian icon [as in the Tokugawa era] to prove my loyalty. After all, I didn't know when what I said would find its way directly to the police or the military police, so I could talk about the war, too, only in the language of slaves. In what I committed to print, there is not a single opportunistic, sycophantic essay, but in the classroom I had to jump through the hoops: that fact damaged my very soul.

—Interview, 1994

Source: Interview with Yanagida Setsuko, in *Taidanshū*, pp. 161–162.

dent's words. That was only the proverbial beginning of the beginning.

I was astonished when in 1942 and 1943 some of the students demanded that we stop using the Western calendar.[6] The lower classes lost the special sense of being higher-school students and gradually became indistinguishable from middle-schoolers. Because the students were more docile, things got easier for the teachers; but I rued the day that higher-school students became indistinguishable from middle-school students. In our day, state control of education extended through middle school, but from higher school on, we were largely outside the realm of state control. The destruction of that distinction meant that from primary school at the bottom to the highest educational institutions at the top, all were now brought completely under the control of the state.

In the opening days of the war with the United States and

---

6. The alternative was the reign-name system: e.g., 1942 as Shōwa 17.

Photo 6.2 Party with students in Ienaga's charge, 1942. Ienaga is in front row, wearing tie. Photo courtesy of Ienaga Saburō.

England, Japan achieved sparkling battlefield victories, one after the other. But from the review Mizuno Hironori had written of the book by Ikezaki Tadataka, I knew that temporary battlefield victories did not necessarily mean final victory; I also knew full well that Japan, exhausted from consecutive wars—the Manchurian Incident and the war with China—couldn't possibly win a war against the United States. So I was utterly unable to rejoice at the initial victories.

The territory Japan occupied expanded day by day, and on the map of Asia hanging in the faculty room, the Japanese flag was drawn in over one place after another. Seeing this, I was battered by uneasiness: "Now that we've seized so much territory, how will we control it?" That was the greatest protest I could express. I could only listen wistfully to the reply of a senior teacher who delighted in the good will of others: "The occupied territories we should develop rapidly; that'll make us strong." Around 1943 I talked over the war with my senior colleague S., now dead, who taught philosophy—the two of us alone in the faculty room, sitting at the hibachi. I joked: "Sinking all these enemy ships— won't that simply increase the reparations we'll have to pay?" Being a serious person, S. was taken aback and took me to task: "Talk like that will get you into serious trouble."

But as the war progressed, I stuck to the realism I had had from the first and on that point experienced no wobbling; I could do so thanks in part to my colleague Uemura Seiji, a teacher of history with me, who arrived at Niigata Higher School at virtually the same time I did. Uemura had been one year ahead of my teacher Sakamoto Tarō, and he had taught at Takayama Higher School. Because two history professors happened to leave Niigata at the same time, Uemura and I arrived to take jobs in Niigata together. While there, I was greatly indebted to Uemura, even in my personal life. Uemura had taken his degree in Chinese history, but he was well-versed in both Japanese and Western history, too, and his knowledge also had true breadth, for he was interested as well in the arts and folklore. He was cynical about the academic world, so he didn't have many strictly academic accomplishments to his credit; still, he had a broad and wide vision of the kind not found among academics. I am indebted to Uemura, too, for teaching me the importance of Yanagita Kunio's ethnography.[7] I

---

7. Yanagita Kunio (1875–1962): folklorist.

remember that Uemura was bold enough to trace the course of the German retreat on the Russian front, in ink, on the map of Europe in the encyclopedia and to say: "Now it's only a matter of time." After I graduated, Japanese history at Tōdai remained under the absolutism of Hiraizumi, an insane academic style prevailed, and serious scholarship had to lie low. When I let slip words that expressed my indignation, Uemura was kind enough to console me: "Well, it can't go on like this for long." He clearly saw through the idea that the war would end soon in victory for Japan. Because I knew a person of such intelligence, I was able to stick to my early insight about the meaning of reports from the battlefield. Even on purely academic issues, too, I learned a lot from Uemura—about Yanagita ethnography and other subjects not taught then in any school. My three years at Niigata meant fleeing the Historiographical Institute, which was a veritable treasurehouse of historical materials, and having to lead a research life in a regional higher school that hadn't even an adequate library. I made the school library my own, read virtually every book in the field, and then suffered from the lack of more materials to work with. If there was a plus side to my three-year life in Niigata, it was entirely thanks to Uemura. It would hardly be exaggerating to say that my stay in Niigata was time spent studying under Uemura's guidance.

Another major plus at Niigata for my life as a scholar was that I had to lecture on the entire history of Japan. In my years at the Historiographical Institute, I could get by doing only ancient history—with a highly textual approach at that. But as a higher-school professor, I had to give lectures on all of Japanese history, from ancient to contemporary. So I had to study early modern and modern history, too; until then I had known nothing at all about these periods. I found early modern history and modern history inexplicably interesting, and since then, I have moved my period of research forward, toward the modern era. It was a time of what might be called crazed Japanism, yet through the study of Japanese history I came to know, paradoxically and in detail, that our ancestors often expended all their effort on the adoption of foreign culture, that in the Meiji era, known as an age of mania for things Western, our ancestors devoted all their energy to the adoption of modern Western culture. In that era of the dark valley I immersed myself in the intellectual history of the adoption of foreign culture and just barely succeeded in avoiding spiritual stagnation. Soon after the war I changed my specialty to modern intellectual history, and this is how I got started in that direction.

My three years in Niigata were a valuable experience for me, but as I've said before, it was a very difficult time. I had to carry on life in a place where as an outsider, with no connections, I faced severe constraints. In addition, I was sickly and, as I had feared, could not take the Niigata climate. My digestive problems gradually worsened; food became particularly difficult to get, and I couldn't select those foods that I could digest easily. So the hardships gradually got worse until finally I made up my mind, submitted my resignation, and came to leave Niigata Higher School. In October 1943, just at the end of the first of the two semesters, I left Niigata and returned to Tokyo. It happened that at the Imperial Academy (predecessor of today's Academy of Japan), Tsuji was supervising the compilation of *The Institutional History of the Imperial House;* help was hard to find in wartime, and he needed editors. He was kind enough to ask me whether I'd like to work there, even if only for a short time. I accepted without a moment's delay.

At the Imperial Academy I had the unexpected opportunity of contact with Minobe Tatsukichi, whom I had long admired. The persecution of 1935 had forced Minobe to resign all his official positions, but the Academy—so the reasoning went—was a purely academic group. So he kept his post at the Academy and was made editor in chief of *The Institutional History of the Imperial House,* then being pressed as an Academy project. It was an unex-

---

I'm a historian, but I've never studied the Meiji Restoration in any serious way. My specialty is intellectual history, and I'm interested in universal human ideas. As human drama the Meiji Restoration is fascinating, but as the pursuit of universal ideas it has no attraction; for me the era of liberty and people's rights [the 1880s] is of interest, with its connections to the history of modern constitutional law. . . . [Someone wrote] that in the Meiji Restoration there are no universal human ideas, and I agree.

—*Interview,* 1992

Source: Interview with Osanai Mieko, in *Taidanshū,* p. 121.

pected treat to work on this project under the supervision of this
senior and eminent scholar whose writings I had long admired.
Two others also took on the actual work of compilation as full-
time employees: Inoue Kiyoshi, then a professor at Kyoto University, and Inoue Mitsusada, then a professor at Tokyo University.[8]
The three of us, all in one room, set to work on the very last stages
of compilation. Among ourselves, we wondered how soon the defeat would come; in the midst of war, our room was a world apart.
But we had only to take one step outside, and there was Japan in
the midst of a fierce war. The shortage of food got worse each day,
so the prime worry for everyone from one day to the next was
getting enough food. Of course, it wasn't all that rough for Inoue
Mitsusada, younger son of a prince, but people like me always
had to think first of all of supplementing—if only slightly—the
family food supply. So when we went to work, we immediately
dropped off our briefcases and hurried to the lunchroom in the
nearby Ueno department store, Matsuzakaya. Here there was a
stew kitchen—stew indistinguishable from soup, and at the official price [not the much higher black market price], they sold one
bowl per person. Several hundred people formed a line that
snaked from the restaurant on the fifth floor down to the third
floor. We waited our turn, and finally, after standing three hours,
we got our one bowl. So by the time we got back to the office, it
was already long past the noon break; there were days when it
almost seemed we went to work in order to go to the soup
kitchen. Scenes like this are probably impossible even to imagine
today, when we are flooded with material goods and, if only we
have the money, can go anywhere and eat our fill of delicious
food. I note this because I would like today's young people, who
have no experience of war, to know what miseries we of the wartime generation remember.

One lasting impression from working on *The Institutional History of the Imperial House* had to do with a facet of Minobe's personality. He was probably Japan's top constitutional scholar, but in
the last analysis, *The Institutional History of the Imperial House* was a
book of history. He would take the first drafts the three of us
wrote and rewrite them completely in his own hand. But when

8. Inoue Kiyoshi (1913–): historian of modern Japan, Marxist. Inoue Mitsusada (1916–1983): historian of ancient Japan.

we saw his rewritten version, there were passages where to our expert eyes the use of historical terms and the like looked a bit strange. Any number of times we said, "Now wouldn't it perhaps look better, sir, if we were to say it this way?" But once he had rewritten things, he brooked no correction. In 1935, when the emperor-organ theory made him the object of a storm of persecution, he said, "No matter what the oppression, I cannot change or alter my academic theories. I cannot retreat even one step from my own theories." When I read that statement in a discussion that appeared in the pages of the *Tōkyō Nichinichi* newspaper, it made a deep impression on me. Now I came to realize for the first time the deeply interesting fact that this attitude was not simply a matter of being true to his beliefs; it was also a matter of character.

If you were knocking around without a job during the war, you were likely to be drafted, yet I got taken on at the Academy. When I think how lucky I was, I think I owed it to them to work there longer; but the next year, 1944, I received an offer from Tokyo Higher Normal School, and after barely half a year at the Academy, I became a professor at Tokyo Higher Normal School. This job came about as a result of the fact that the late Nakagawa Kazuo made a special trip to my home and, showing the greatest confidence in me, invited me to take the job. At the time I had also heard from Takeoka Katsuya of Kyushu University that he wished me to go there, and for a while negotiations went forward to that end. But after a good deal of back and forth, I decided finally on the job at Tokyo Higher Normal School. That is how I came to the Ōtsuka campus, where I have taught now for more than twenty-five years.

However, after taking the job at Ōtsuka, I taught barely one week. I had been teaching for one week when all of a sudden year-round mobilization was instituted, and the students all disappeared. And I had to go to work in shifts to supervise work at the Kamata airplane factory; that was where the history and geography students were mobilized. In 1945 the aerial bombardment of Tokyo intensified. In the great raid of March 10, the city center was reduced to ashes, and more than 70,000 residents died horrible deaths. By sheer chance I was sleeping that night in the dorm in Kamata.

Sometime in the fall of 1944 my health had gone bad, and I

still had a slight fever and diarrhea. The extreme torment of food shortages, the intensification of the air raids, the shortage of medicine, and the rest: the unfavorable conditions accumulated, and my symptoms simply would not go away. In this sickly state I did my shifts at the Kamata factory. On the night of March 10, in a stiff wind, I made the rounds of the neighborhood of the dormitory on the lookout for firebombs, and my condition worsened. Nakagawa took sympathy on me for my illness and permitted me to leave Tokyo to devote myself to recuperation. I felt I owed an apology to my elders and colleagues who were suffering under the year-round mobilization. But in Tokyo, there was no food, and I could not sleep peacefully at night, so I could not hope to recuperate there. I left for Sendai, my wife's home, and became an invalid.

I had just signed a contract for *History of Early Yamato-e*, which I had already finished; the typesetting was 80 percent complete, and galley proofs were on the way. At this point, in the great Tokyo air raid of May 25, the type that was 80 percent set and the manuscript all went up in flames. Learning in Sendai that years of research had been reduced to naught, I was deeply saddened. After the defeat I returned to Tokyo, and to my surprise I learned that the first galley proofs and the first draft of the manuscript, including the portions not yet set into type, had been in the air

---

I myself had no direct contact with the reality of colonial rule, but when my wife was at Japan Women's University, she had Korean and Chinese friends in the dormitory. At Dairen [in Manchuria] the authorities distributed rice to Japanese, but to Chinese they distributed only kaoliang. A friend from Dairen came to Tokyo as a foreign student but even then got no rice ration book. My wife was on the dorm council, and they became friends when they worked together to get her a rice ration book. Even today that discrimination makes her see red. Even though we are husband and wife, we think very differently, but on important matters like this, we see eye to eye, so we haven't gotten divorced (smile). This year we'll celebrate our golden wedding anniversary.

—Interview, 1994

Source: Interview with Yanagida Setsuko, in *Taidanshū*, pp. 159–160.

raid shelter at my home and were undamaged, so after the war I was able to publish it. What unexpected good fortune! I survived the grim war, escaping not simply with my life but with my manuscripts, too, in virtually complete form. If only for that reason, when I think of the fate of my generation, far more able and richly talented than I, most of whom lost their lives in the fires of war, I have an unbearable sense that I can never atone for having survived. The day of defeat came, and I had never been to the front lines, nor, though exposed at home to many air raids, had I ever seen a single dead body. So although I belong to the wartime generation, I cannot say I know the true horror of war. Still, even I know acutely, at a level that is more than skin-deep, the sufferings of war, how war mercilessly destroys people, body and soul. In this sense I am first and foremost a person who bears in his heart the scars of war. This, too, was one of the experiences that shaped my postwar life.

As a last wartime memory, I want to say a word about my relations with Tanabe Hajime.[9] I've already mentioned that in 1932, as a result of reading Tanabe's *Outline of the Sciences,* I experienced an intellectual revolution. Thereafter, I received much stimulus from Tanabe's scholarship. I did not become a Marxist, yet I also escaped the morality of traditional Japanism, and what filled the void in my heart was the philosophy of Tanabe. As I've already said, the strongest influences on me came not from professors

---

[T]he absence of an awareness among historians of the role of women in history was the result of being constrained by social conditions centering on the ie [family] system of patriarchal control that lasted from the Edo period into modern times. Hence the opening of eyes to see women's history could not take place without aspirations for a society in which males and females are equal, linked with the destruction of that patriarchal ie system, or a women's liberation movement.

—Essay, 1985

Source: Ienaga, "Nihon joseishi to no meguriai," *Rekishigaku kenkyū* 542 (June 1985); in *Ienaga Saburō shū,* vol. 16, p. 241.

---

9. Tanabe Hajime (1885–1962): philosopher.

whose classes I took but from other scholars, indirectly, through their writing. I like to count Tanabe, too, as one of the teachers outside the classroom to whom I am greatly indebted.

The publisher Kōbundō issued my first book, *The Development of the Logic of Negation in Japanese Intellectual History.* (In fact, this book was published thanks to the good offices of Takayama Iwao, then an assistant professor at Kyoto University.[10] Unfortunately, Takayama and I came thereafter to hold opposing intellectual views, but when I think of the distant past, it is with the deepest of feelings.) Before publication I sent offprints of the journal articles on which it was based to Tanabe, long my model. To my surprise I received a very kind reply. Even now I remember vividly how overjoyed I was. Thereafter, he and I exchanged an occasional letter, and finally it came about that with his endorsement I received a scholarship from the Fūjukai, set up with funds donated by Iwanami Shigeo. Immediately thereafter, I was appointed professor at Niigata Normal Higher School, and to Tanabe's very strict way of thinking, that meant I had to resign the scholarship after only a few months. But I had not been his student and had never met him, and I was profoundly grateful for his good offices. After I left Niigata and returned to Tokyo, I made use of the time before I began my job at the Academy to take a trip to Kyoto. I toured Katsura Detached Palace for the first time and then met Tanabe for the first time, visiting him at his home in the Yoshida section of town; for about two hours I inquired about various matters. The date was October 8, 1943. After returning to Tokyo, I set down the day's dialogue from memory, and I have that record today—under the self-important title, "Record of a Dialogue in the Western Capital." That was the only time I was able to speak directly with him on matters of scholarship and ideas. It is a very inflated parallel, but to myself I like to compare it with the night Kamo Mabuchi and Motoori Norinaga met at Matsuzaka.[11]

What attracted me to the philosophy of Tanabe was his coming to grips heroically with actual problems, trying to explain the essence of the world in terms of praxis. The then-popular philoso-

10. Takayama Iwao (1905–1993).
11. Kamo Mabuchi (1697–1769); Motoori Norinaga (1730–1801). They met in 1763, a meeting that had a profound effect on the younger Norinaga.

phy of Nishida Kitarō,[12] I realized, was on a scale one step larger than Tanabe's philosophy, and deep meditation lay behind it, yet I never felt that much attraction to it. Again, the philosophy of Watsuji Tetsurō, who moved to Tōdai from Kyoto University while I was a student, sparked a great early interest, and I read many of his books with pleasure. But with Watsuji's philosophy I sensed a strong aura somehow of play, and even though I came close to being a fan of Watsuji's philosophy, I wasn't a devotee. By contrast, in the philosophy of Tanabe, there was a strong quest for truth, and, unlike Watsuji, who seemed to be amusing himself with philosophy as a pastime, I sensed vividly, even between the printed lines of his works, that Tanabe was absorbed absolutely and totally in philosophy; I was struck by the force of his philosophy. To be sure, beginning about 1940 his philosophy gradually came to overemphasize race and state, and by the time he came to speak of things like "the logic of species," I could not avoid feeling a slight unease. As I have said before, my own ideas in this era had, if anything, turned their back on reality and, sinking in the direction of the internal/religious, moved in the direction opposite the nationalist trend of the times. Still, until the last I was powerless to end my attraction to Tanabe's philosophy. Different from the racial philosophies of the other nationalists, "the logic of species" took as its axis the mutual mediation of three entities—species, class, and individual; I read it, despite the emphasis on species, as upholding to the very end the relative independence of the individual. For example, the first time I read "The Logic of Species—World Schema," published in the October 1935 issue (no. 235) of *Studies in Philosophy*, there were statements like these:

> For individuals, belonging to a species is not a matter of an inorganic and transparent relation. Through the negation or affirmation of the species by individuals, the species itself changes once again. That is, the actual way whereby the species is renewed sets individuals in a relation of mutuality with the species. It is not simply an undifferentiated relationship between individual and species. To think so is nothing other than an unmediated intuitionism that completely disregards individuals as actual subjects.

---

12. Nishida Kitarō (1870–1945): philosopher.

Again:

> Through the direct unification of the communities that are
> their bases, races constrain individuals, and they are to be per-
> ceived as entities that through the strength of their historical
> traditions deny individuals their spontaneity. But no one
> takes humankind to be an immediate unity having that power
> of denial vis-à-vis individuals. On the contrary, the so-called
> way of humaneness that governs humankind is a negation of
> the direct unity of the species in that it governs general rela-
> tions among equal individuals transcending the specificities of
> species/race. Unlike the species, which stands in direct opposi-
> tion to individuals, the way of humaneness has on the con-
> trary the characteristic of being an unmediated relation that
> arises by liberating individuals from the duress of the species
> and enabling them to stand free.

I took these passages to mean that Tanabe upheld to the end
the independence of the individual. On this single point of upholding the independence of the individual, I maintained my
trust in Tanabe's philosophy to the last.

Kuno Osamu,[13] a disciple of Tanabe with whom I became ac-
quainted after the war, told me, "That's a misreading on your
part. In Tanabe's philosophy the issue of the organization of individuals—that is, bourgeois solidarity—completely drops out; your
reading of Tanabe philosophy is a misreading." But as Tsurumi
Shunsuke[14] argues in his book *The Right to Misunderstand,* people
sometimes learn more via misunderstanding than what is written
in a book. By reading Tanabe's philosophy in what Kuno calls a
misreading, I was able amid the storm of extreme nationalism to
find philosophical support for my post-1932 liberalism. To be fair,
it cannot be denied that Tanabe's philosophy came very, very close
to a statism that accommodated itself to the trend of the times,
but he did not betray my high expectations: already toward the
end of the war Tanabe engaged in self-criticism of his own statist
tendency and finally turned back to a philosophy of repentance.
Thereby he was able to avoid the superficial affirmation of "the
Greater East Asian War" of those such as Takayama Iwao and

---

13. Kuno Osamu (1910–): journalist; professor.
14. Tsurumi Shunsuke (1922–): philosopher, critic.

Kōsaka Masaaki.[15] So I'm not sure mine was necessarily a fundamental misunderstanding of Tanabe philosophy. When we look at his postwar conduct and speech, too, there is room for criticism, but still, I think that his fundamental path was not sheer lunacy.

As I have described, I was so useless and incompetent I might have been born by mistake. Still, I had personal contact with outstanding men of thought who will live in history—Minobe Tatsukichi and Tanabe Hajime—and in my own generation I have had outstanding men of thought and research as friends—Maruyama Masao and others (unfortunately, there will be no time to speak of them in this volume). Both counts are cause for heartfelt rejoicing.

Historical consciousness too is a product of history . . . In the case of women's history . . . for a long time history was all history of males only, and women were treated merely as appendages. Because history equaled the history of males, unless we established a separate category of women's history, the role and status of women in history would disappear entirely.

I am a Japanese researcher who knows only Japan, so I write not about women's history in the breadth of human history but only about women's history in Japan; in premodern Japanese history, it goes without saying, but even in modern history up to the fifteen-year war, the unconscious historical view prevailed that history equaled men's history. So there was not even much awareness of the need to establish a field of Japanese women's history, and the start of basic research in Japanese women's history came only in the postwar era.

—Essay, 1985

Source: Ienaga, "Nihon joseishi," *Ienaga Saburō shū*, vol. 16, pp. 238–239.

---

15. Kōsaka Masaaki (1900–1969): literary scholar.

7

MY STATE OF MIND IN THE PERIOD
IMMEDIATELY AFTER THE DEFEAT

From the first, I had had no illusions about the war, and as the end approached, my despair became complete. After I moved to Sendai to recuperate, my aged parents, too, decided to come to Sendai in order to get out of the city; they rented a single room in a temple in a farm village barely five miles from Sendai. Once, asking too much of my frail body, I went to them. To my eyes, accustomed only to city life, the rice paddies in their early summer green, wholly removed from the fierce war situation, were truly beautiful. Had it been a time of peace, this beautiful country scene would have brought me great pleasure. But I knew that the destruction of my native land was now merely a matter of time, and even this beautiful country scene left me unmoved. My soul was as cold as ice; I had fallen into a state of torpor: I had lost not only my sensitivity to the beauties of nature but also my hope as a human being to survive.

At the time I had absolutely no idea that anyone was carrying on stalwart antiwar activity: Yanaihara Tadao and Masaki Hiroshi, who had expressed their beliefs more than fully and continued to publish one-person magazines, not bowing to the strongest press restrictions; Tokuda Kyūichi and Shiga Yoshio, who suffered in prison for ten years and, keeping the faith by not committing apostasy, waited for their day to come; people organizing the anti-war movement in China.[1] I myself had been unable to do anything at all to liberate the people from the sufferings of war and

---

1. Yanaihara Tadao (1893–1961): economist, educator, pacifist. Masaki Hiroshi (1896–1975): lawyer, activist. Tokuda Kyūichi (1894–1953): founder of the Japan Communist Party. Shiga Yoshio (1901–1989): member, Communist Party.

could only watch from the sidelines as my country died, and I suffered every day the pains of illness as well, so I was driven into a mood of nihilism. For that very reason, August 15, 1945, marked for me the end of an era tinged with madness, and I welcomed it with great joy. The majority of well-meaning Japanese, who had given the war their heartfelt cooperation, were said to have listened to the emperor's broadcast sadly, tears flowing, but we learned later that a good many heaved a great sigh of relief at this broadcast, and some even showed heartfelt joy, with others among them celebrating by drinking to the defeat. I was one of this last group.

I thought a harrowing situation might develop—that even after the defeat, the military, not shying away from a last stand at home, might carry on a guerrilla war at home, so that the home islands, too, would become a battlefield, and my sense of despair deepened. Fortunately, this prediction proved false. We learned much later that for a while after the announcement, some people at Atsugi and other air force units called for a continuation of the war, but the military I thought might continue its armed resistance laid down its weapons just like that, and the Occupation army landed without bloodshed. Fortunately, this was not what I had forecast—a miscalculation to rejoice over. But in fact, I had despaired over the current condition of the state and turned my back completely on politics, immersing myself exclusively in problems of the spirit, internal problems, so I was utterly unable to judge the direction in which postwar Japan should be reconstructed or how the international and domestic scene might develop.

With the defeat, many of my friends turned immediately in new directions and undertook constructive activities in high spirits, but I could only take in the defeat passively and rejoice at the termination of the terrible war and the end of the era of the dark valley. In retrospect, that is a source of sincere shame.

Since our school days people like me had experienced severe restraints on freedom of expression and had undergone repeated hardships. Then, right after the Occupation began, the Occupa- tion army ordered the Japanese government to abolish all the internal security legislation—publication law, law governing access to paper for newspapers, and the rest, and at least in regard to domestic issues, freedom of expression was guaranteed wholly.

In the war, Japanese learned firsthand that the military never protects the people. Not only starting a war that was hopeless—[the Sugiyama memo's] "we can fight for two years but thereafter things are utterly unclear"—but also calling for "decisive battle in the home islands" right up to the atomic bombs and the Soviet Union's entry into the war, when no one could hope for victory, when if they had stopped the war millions of their countrymen would have survived: from these facts, isn't it crystal clear that the military considers the lives of the people as so much worthless rubbish?

—November 1, 1980

Source: Ienaga, "Guntai wa kokumin no seimei o mamoru ka," Asahi, November 1, 1980; in Ienagashū, vol. 12, p. 279.

For people like me, that was a great harvest from the lost war, and we couldn't help rejoicing from the bottom of our hearts. In my school days we could not even own complete texts of the classic cultural works of Japan—for example, the works of Ihara Saikaku or Tamenaga Shunsui.[2] In the case of these works of the Tokugawa era, all that was permitted was publication of the woodblock versions—probably because the average person could not read the anomalous cursive script. In the case of editions set in movable type, deletions dotted the page; in the case of works like Saikaku's *Tales of the Floating World* in particular, there were pages where more than half the text had been deleted. As for works of the period after 1868 and ideas of liberty and people's rights, socialism and communism, or peace and antiwar ideologies, either there were deletions or you simply couldn't get hold of the texts legally. I have never been so happy as when such "proscribed books" began to appear openly in the stores. Before, classics like the works of Saikaku could still be published with deletions, but there had been no way legally, for example, to publish things like *Suetsumuhana*, the collection of lewd and humorous verse, and illegal books and manuscripts could be read only in secret, among small groups of aficionados. The abolition of the peace preservation laws brought this situation, too, to an end, and for the first

---

2. Ihara Saikaku (1642–1693): poet, writer. Tamenaga Shunsui (1790–1843): writer.

time printed editions appeared openly in the bookstores. I had never thought I would live to see the day when we could buy and read *Suetsumuhana* openly, so my feelings as I held these books in my own hands are impossible to describe.

I am digressing a bit, but one often hears it said that the freedom of the postwar era went too far, that we were inundated with "bad books," that juvenile delinquency increased for that reason; so restrictions on "bad books" were issued, and with mothers in the lead, movements to purge "bad books" were organized. Holding the memories I do, I cannot go along with movements led by private citizens to purge bad books. I wouldn't want to show juveniles many of the books flooding the cities today—that I won't deny. However, there are important problems in this world, and they can't be solved merely by saying that these books must be suppressed because they're injurious to juveniles. I know too well from my prewar experience the kind of wintry situation that sets in when all "bad books" have been banished completely.

What's more, it isn't as easy as those who would purge "bad books" think to say which are "bad books" and which "good books." The prewar approved texts that set us up for the war and prevented the emergence of ways of thinking critical of the war— weren't they the worst of all "bad books"? As for the publications that are now being called "bad books," people don't read them thinking to learn anything. If the books one reads looking for knowledge and ideas do not transmit the truth, or if they inculcate into the unsuspecting minds of many a mindset that truckles to evil authority, financial or political, then they are incomparably more harmful than the "bad books." Which are today's truly

---

When I was young, I didn't see many movies, but in middle age I watched a good many raptly: Western classics—all of Chaplin's work—"Modern Times" and the rest, this was a revival, and "Under the Roofs of Paris," and, among Japanese films, "Till We Meet Again," "Ikiru," and the rest. The years after the defeat were great years in Japanese and Western filmmaking, weren't they!

—1992

Source: Interview with Osanai Mieko, January 20, 1992; in *Taidanshū*, p. 126.

worst "bad books"? One needs to ponder that question long and coolly. When, as a result of the defeat, the "bad books" that had been proscribed before the war flooded the stores, I experienced tremendous joy; I felt that surviving the war was worthwhile for that reason alone. This I avow here explicitly.

It was also a great joy for me that freedom of expression was guaranteed, in the first instance by decrees of the Occupation army, and that as a result, research in Japanese history, which had suffered under particularly tight restrictions on freedom of expression, suddenly regained its vigor. I don't remember being impressed as deeply when the Constitution of Japan was established and the Meiji Constitution revised wholesale and fundamental human rights guaranteed. Already before the establishment of the constitution, as one facet of Occupation policy, actual guarantees of freedom of expression had been instituted, so that is one reason I was unable to recognize the epoch-making significance of the new constitution right at the start, at its enactment. Nor was I aware then of the restrictions on freedom of expression through such means as the press code and radio pacts that forbade destructive criticism of Occupation policies—that was another great blind spot of mine.

As I've already mentioned, I had done nothing to bring about the conclusion of the war, and I was unable to embark immediately on constructive activity to rebuild postwar Japan. Not only that, but I could only feel disgust at what did emerge. The journalistic world had continued until just yesterday to spout "Carry the sacred war on to victory!" Now it did a complete about-face and, under the instruction of the Occupation army, it couldn't find enough hours in the day for singing the praises of "democracy." As public opinion and intellectual opinion changed so completely, indeed almost flip-flopped, I couldn't follow meekly along. And the slogan of "democracy," which, properly speaking, merited one's wholehearted support: I saw it as nothing but hollow cant, and I was unable to suppress the feeling that it was simply the flip side of the wartime militarism.

In the academic domain of history, too, the school of historical materialism that until then had suffocated under severe persecution suddenly came to life and showed such vigor that it came virtually to rule a vast number of scholars. But many of its arguments were crudely formulaic, and for that reason and others, I

> I recognized that, unfortunately, the war dead died, frankly, in vain—very coldhearted phrase though that is, and I thought that we should consider how to give meaning to these meaningless deaths. How? By working to keep such a tragedy from happening again; then and only then will the deaths of all the victims be not meaningless deaths but revered sacrifices. . . . [M]erely to beautify deaths in and for themselves is very dangerous. . . .
>
> I had been a bystander [during the war] . . . and immediately after the defeat I was again a bystander—in part because I felt the manner in which the progressive forces called the people to task was very inhumane. I remember reading somewhere this rebuttal to the "progressives" from those who collaborated in the war effort: if they knew that the war was an aggression, why hadn't they let us know earlier? During the war, of course, there was in fact no freedom of expression, but although the progressives owed a debt for having been unable to act effectively to prevent the war, after the war they avoided that issue and focused only on criticizing the collaborators. . . . I was not under attack, but I felt uneasy somehow with that behavior. That's an important reason why for a while after the war I merely observed the democratization from outside.
>
> —1977
>
> Source: Ienaga and Hidaka Rokurō, "Rekishi to sekinin," Gendai to shisō 30 (December 1977); in Ienagashū, vol. 12, pp. 155–156.

could not help feeling unease with a large part of the postwar historical world. Indeed, I took a critical stance toward this new postwar development. An evaluation of the profession entitled "Hopes for a New Positivism" that appeared in Shohyō 4, published in May 1947, shows my opinions at the time. On the one hand, I criticize sharply the old positivist history—"the lazy and pusillanimous positivism that up till now has constructed its nest in orthodox history and that tries to camouflage its spiritual poverty by sheer numbers of citations to sources." On the other hand, I also carve out a position in reaction to the historical view of postwar conceptual formalism. The next year I published a short essay, "An Unpositivism to Be Wary of—The Latest Trend in the World of History," in Arts and Sciences News for March 15, 1948; there, in particular reference to the argument in ancient history over lineal communal societies, I expressed a negative attitude toward the theories of the historical materialists. In the September 5–15, 1949, issue of *Tokyo University of Education Newspaper* I published a short essay, "On a Second Look at Great People in History," and there I expressed much the same feeling, to the effect that "we should not make snap judgments."

At the time, the community of historians looked at me as the ringleader of reaction, not only because of these statements. A second reason was that in 1946 I became a member of the editorial committee of the new certified text in Japanese history, *The Progress of the Country* [*Kuni no ayumi*], a project being urged under the leadership of the information bureau of the Occupation's popular education section. *The Progress of the Country* was put together on demand in barely one month's time, with absolutely no preparation, by a staff assembled out of the blue, so it is not without reason that its workmanship left a good deal to be desired.

In the sea to the east of the Asiatic continent there are islands which stretch from north to south in a long thin line. These are the islands of Japan where we live. The heat and cold are not extreme; rain falls in good measure; the trees and grasses grow thick, and the scenery in each of the four seasons has a different appearance.

It was in very ancient times that our ancestors settled down in this country. We do not know just when it was, but without a doubt it was at least several thousand years ago. All over the world, in times when culture was not developed, man still did not know how to use metal. He made tools of stone and used them. This period is known as the Stone Age. Occasionally when we are walking on the warm, southern side of hills we see shells scattered about, gleaming white in the fields. These are salt-water and fresh-water clams which the people of those days collected, ate and then piled up. We call these shell mounds. From shell mounds, besides shells, the bones of fish and tools ordinarily used by the people of those days are dug out. From these finds we can tell how the people of ancient times lived.

—The beginning of The Progress of the Country

Source: Opening of *Kuni no ayumi*, in *Nihon kyōkasho taikei—kindai-hen*, ed. Kaigo Tokiomi and Naka Arata (Tokyo: Kōdansha, 1962), vol. 20, pp. 386f. The translation is by John Caiger, in "Ienaga Saburō and the First Postwar Japanese History Textbook," *Modern Asian Studies* 3, no. 1 (1969): 12.

Moreover, the great majority of that staff were positivist historians with no sense of politics. It is cause for embarrassment today that I, in particular, could do no better than that—at that time I was politically blind; but in fact it couldn't have been helped. The book was criticized by people in the progressive camp as if it was written with the political intent of offering positive support to the old order. But if I may plead my own case, that is a false charge. It's only that if you ask positivist historians with no political smarts to do the writing, that's all they'll produce.

Still, it is hard to deny that as the point of departure for the new postwar education in Japanese history, *The Progress of the Country* did not close the books on the old view of history. As one who shared responsibility for writing it, I have no choice but to accept that criticism.

But *The Progress of the Country* was only a stop-gap, undertaken in order to fill a transitional need. The work of educational reform soon went forward, and as it did, wholesale reform in Japanese history education made even more progress; in particular, the epoch-making 1951 code of academic ethics was completed: that is truly cause for rejoicing. I take some small consolation in the fact that even the botched *The Progress of the Country* did have meaning—as a failed experiment. I haven't the slightest intention of trying to exculpate myself, but let me note one thing while I'm at it. At the time the work was entrusted to me, the supervisor of the Ministry of Education's book division had already done up a draft, and that draft apparently did not satisfy the intent of the Occupation army's reform of historical education. It was on this account that we researchers from outside the Ministry were brought together, and a fundamental recompilation was undertaken. We learned all this only afterward. Before beginning the rewriting, I was handed the supervisor's draft for my assigned section—ancient history—and asked to stick to the draft as much as possible. I read it, and it did start with the Neolithic Age; but a little later it treated the myths from the *Kojiki* and the *Nihongi,* myths that are not historical fact, at some length. I agreed almost entirely with Tsuda Sōkichi's thorough-going critique of those two texts, so I decided to excise those parts entirely and stick exclusively to objective historical fact from the Neolithic Age on down. Up until then, the world of history education had considered it a matter of course to begin with the tales of the age of

Q: Looking at your writings, I think the real reason *The Progress of the Country* failed was not necessarily what you've just said [Ienaga had just given three reasons: lack of experience with primary school education, lack of time, and his own failings], so let me ask again, with reference to your writings: on page 130 of *One Historian's Odyssey,* four lines from the bottom, you say the real reason *The Progress of the Country* was a failure was, "Ask positivist historians with no political smarts to do the writing, and that's all they'll produce." In short, because textbooks written by positivists are failures, because it failed because of lack of political smarts—I think that is the true failure. Would you care to comment?

A: This passage was not written to say that. Although *The Progress of a Country* was criticized as if it were an attempt to support the old order or was written with political intent, those criticisms are wide of the mark—that was my point. . . .

Q: Then in the ninth line on p. 130, eighth word from the end, it says, "Moreover, the great majority of that staff were positivist historians with no sense of politics. It is cause for embarrassment today that I, in particular, could do no better than that—at that time I was politically blind; but in fact it couldn't have been helped." And then it continues much farther on . . .

A: Yes.

Q: . . . that it was a failure—isn't that the point?

A: That is one of the reasons included in the third reason I mentioned earlier [his own failings]. I didn't write this passage limiting everything to "this reason alone," so the main point here is an antithesis to that criticism, so I emphasized that aspect; it wasn't the only aspect.

Q: Why—despite the fact that this is an important point on which you placed heavy emphasis—did you omit it from your earlier testimony?

A: No, that . . .

Q: You had no particular motive?

A: No particular motive. This book is in print, and anyone can read it. I had no motive to hide anything.

> *—Exchange with opposition counsel at the textbook trial, 1969*

Source: Under cross-examination at lawsuit #2, Tokyo District Court (Judge Sugimoto presiding), August 28, 1969; in *Shōgenshū,* pp. 169–170.

the gods and of Emperor Jimmu, so even this represented a major change.

At present, in my suit contesting the legality of textbook certification, I state that one of the Ministry of Education's illegal actions is its deletion from my text of the true nature of the stories of the age of the gods and of the recounting of the first several emperors, beginning with Emperor Jimmu, that are found in the *Kojiki* and the *Nihongi*. At the time I wrote the first postwar textbook on Japanese history, I eliminated all the tales that are not recognized as objective narration of historical truth. These two actions had their origin in precisely the same approach, and on that issue, my position is the same now as it was then.

As for postwar guilt, it is precisely the same issue in formalistic terms as wartime guilt. . . . In the historical process there are always choices, even if conditions restrict them to a narrow sphere, and the results differ according to the choices you make.

In order to make the right decisions, you need first of all a correct, objective consciousness, and next you need the inner strength to stick with the choices you make. If the two—the intellectual and the moral—are not conjoined, nothing happens. To unite both and stick with them, you must have both at the same time: a correct reading of the social-historical moment and the passion to commit yourself to the future that that correct consciousness enables you to foresee. Otherwise you get swept away by the trend of the times.

—1977

Source: Ienaga and Hidaka Rokurō, "Rekishi to sekinin," pp. 159–160.

8

THE BEGINNING OF THE REVERSE
COURSE AND THE MATURING OF MY
SOCIAL CONSCIOUSNESS

At the time of the outbreak of the Manchurian Incident, I was a first-year student in higher school and for a while immediately thereafter I was in danger of sliding in the direction of militarism; I have already described that situation. Immediately after the defeat, I faced another—albeit not so acute—intellectual crisis. During the war many "old liberals" of the prewar era and the scholars and critics of my generation had held firmly to a critical posture, but amid the changed circumstances after the war, some of them turned militantly anticommunist, forming an ideological bloc. Had my own frame of mind of the several years after the defeat gotten worse, I, too, might have been in danger of joining them.

Immediately after the Manchurian Incident, most intellectuals swung to the right, but I passed them going the other way, discarding statism and being reborn intellectually; I have already covered those developments in detail. In the postwar intellectual crisis, too, I was lucky and escaped from this second crisis by going against the trend. It was not only that I was unable to align myself with the intellectuals who flip-flopped immediately after the war. As I watched the Occupation army carry out war crimes trials and a purge of public officials and as I saw the wartime ruling class collapse, I had no particular sympathy for them, but I couldn't work myself up to kick people when they were down. During the war I had abhorred the militarists, but that didn't mean I should attack a routed enemy. Such were my true, unfeigned feelings.

However, a new situation arose that caused my feelings to change. This was the reverse course (a term we hardly use any more), which began about 1950–1951 and became pronounced at about the time of the signing of the San Francisco peace treaty. At first, the Occupation army had devoted all its energy to the democratization and demilitarization of Japan, but as the Cold War intensified and in particular with the sudden outbreak of the Korean War, it altered its earlier Occupation policies sharply and came to pursue with great urgency a policy of reintegrating Japan into the anticommunist military camp. It called a halt to the trial of former militarists and others who were leaders during the war and lifted the restrictions on most of those who had been purged. At the same time, it began once again to suppress communists—it had been the Occupation army itself that at the start of the Occupation had liberated the communists from jail!—and carried out one after the other, beginning with the red purge, policies that once again reduced the Communist Party to virtually illegal status.

To be sure, the democratization of Japan had been advanced under an Occupation over which the United States had sole control, so it had contained the seeds of that tendency to anticommunism from the first. I had no sense of politics at the time and couldn't grasp this turnabout in 1949 and 1950, but 1952 brought the enactment of the law against destructive activities, and I became aware—belatedly and for the first time—of the turnabout. This time there was great concern even among historians that the

---

Ienaga's lawsuits bore the heavy burden of Japan's modern and contemporary history. In particular, that it was not possible to end the Pacific War through the efforts of the Japanese people, that the Occupation in fact was a solely U. S. enterprise, that during the Cold War American policy changed, and that the old guard revived. It was in terms of the value system arising from those events that Ienaga was requested to revise his text.

—Younger colleague, 1998

Source: Emura Eiichi, in "Zadankai: Kyōkasho saiban shien undō no sanjūninen," in *Rekishi no hōtei*, p. 188.

enactment of this law might lead once again to the suppression of academic freedom, and on July 22 of that year, under the auspices of four academic associations, a joint scholarly conference took place in a lecture hall at Tokyo University; the topic—"On Freedom of Historical Research." This conference attempted to express via scholarly presentations the opposition of historians to the enactment of this law. That these four very different scholarly associations should join in sponsoring this conference for the common good was unprecedented and deserving of notice.

The History Association of Tokyo University of Education was one of the four sponsoring groups, and at the meeting of conference organizers, the role of speaker from Tokyo University of Education fell to me. I had not been particularly active before, but I agreed to deliver this lecture; in a sense, this set me on the course I was to follow thereafter. It was not simply the resuscitation of peace preservation legislation; the trend toward reaction was strong in the world of history education, too. Arguing that the postwar reforms of civics education, particularly history, had gone too far, a movement arose from the conservative camp to revise the code of academic conduct in a retrogressive direction. For me, a historian, this hit even closer to home than the enactment of the law against destructive activities. As one who shared in the work of compiling *The Progress of the Country*—despite all the criticism, still the first postwar attempt to change the teaching of history—I simply could not stand by silently and watch a movement grow that aimed to call a halt to the postwar reforms in education.

In August of that year I consulted with four other historians—Konishi Shirō, Tōyama Shigeki, Satō Shinichi, and Inoue Mitsusada,[1] and we agreed we had to do something. And so, seeking the endorsement of as many historians as possible, we tried to express our opposition to changes for the worse in history education. A call to action went out over our five signatures, and we organized a group of twenty-four sponsors. Under the auspices of this group, we sent an appeal to a wide range of historians and got the endorsement of some 260. Nishioka Toranosuke[2] and several representatives presented the text of the declaration these people

---

1. Konishi Shirō (1914–1996), Tōyama Shigeki (1914–   ), Satō Shinichi (1916–   ): historians.
2. Nishioka Toranosuke (1895–1970): historian.

> There is one way, we often hear, in which Japan was fortunate—that un-like Germany and Korea, Japan was not cut up into pieces; but it's not the case that Japan was not divided: don't forget that Japan proper and Okinawa are still divided [in 1969]. And the agonies the Okinawans have suffered during these twenty-four years under the control of another na-tion. . . . And these shocking things [crimes by U. S. soldiers immune from prosecution by the civilian government] happen to our countrymen. More-over Okinawa is being used as a base for a most brutal war of aggression against Vietnam. And from there the fearsome bombers fly. . . . By no means can we say, "The postwar has ended." . . . Not only has the post-war not come to an end, we are now in the process of returning to the prewar state of affairs.
>
> —1969
>
> Source: Ienaga, "Sengo wa owatta ka" (1969), in Sensō to kyōiku o megutte (Hōsei daigaku, 1973), pp. 69, 80.

had signed to the Ministry of Education, and the minister of edu-cation took it under advisement. The contents of that declaration are as follows:

Until 1945 and defeat in the Pacific War, instruction in Japa-nese history in general education in Japan was carried out un-scientifically and based on narrow statist ideas; as historians, we feel painfully our responsibility for not being able to pre-vent that from happening.

In this sense, we attach great significance to the fact that the reforms of education in Japanese history carried out since 1946 have marked an end to the earlier unscientific and paro-chial instruction in Japanese history. Because they were car-ried out under the Occupation and for various other reasons, these reforms were not necessarily ideal; but we believe firmly that the basic spirit of scientific instruction in Japanese his-tory must be maintained into the future at all costs.

Hence we oppose firmly all attempts, even the slightest, to swing the policies of instruction in Japanese history in the schools back in the prewar direction. In addition, we ask those responsible to see that the code of academic ethics and the standards for textbook certification under no circumstances be changed with that purpose in mind.

In the next year, 1954, an attempt was made to enact two education laws, and draft legislation concerning the maintenance of educational neutrality was presented to the Diet, as was the proposed revision of the state employee law to prohibit teachers from engaging in political activities. I considered that these, too, were threats to academic freedom and the freedom of ideas, so I cooperated with friends on the faculty of Tokyo University of Education and worked out a plan to get the agreement of a majority of university people throughout the country to issue a declaration. Fortunately, this effort also gained the endorsement of eight hundred people from about seventy universities, and we submitted the declaration to the Diet. The text of that statement ran as follows:

> An attempt is being made to take special legislative action to prohibit political activity on the part of university and high school teachers and prohibit political advocacy by teachers in grades one through nine.
>   We hold this attempt to be a grave infringement on the freedoms of thought, speech, and scholarship that the constitution guarantees. The Fundamental Law of Education states clearly that in conformity with the spirit of the constitution and without submitting to inappropriate control, teachers should carry out lively educational activities to educate the next generation to become bearers of the democratic state.
>   Hence we must express our total opposition to measures like these that use laws to restrict the freedom of education and even involve the danger of threatening freedom of academic research.
>   We ask the careful consideration of all parties.

At the time of the enactment of the two education laws, the Nihon hyōronsha magazine *Hōritsu jihō* happened to come and ask me for an essay. This was my first opportunity to write on legal issues. My essay, entitled "On the 'Neutrality of Education' and the Constitution," appeared in the April 1954 issue; I criticized the report of the Council for Education that became the stimulus for the two education laws and spoke positively of the intent of Article 9 of the constitution to uphold ideas of peace. This was my debut essay publicizing my firm opinions on a constitutional issue.

As I stated earlier, at the time of its promulgation I did not

> Even if you hide [atrocities] from the Japanese people, the people in the other country know about them, so for the two countries to have amicable relations in the future, it is not good at all if the other country knows about the wrongs done them and the perpetrator doesn't. For example, despite the fact that it was the territory of a neutral state, Portugal, Japan occupied the island of Timor. The postwar generation doesn't know the first thing about it, but it's all there in Portuguese textbooks. The side that suffered doesn't forget. The side that inflicted the suffering forgets. Even worse in the case of a country like China, on which we inflicted large-scale damage. . . . [A Japanese Protestant minister of the nineteenth century] said that true patriotism lies in recognizing head-on one's country's mistakes and reflecting on them thoroughly; I think in education, too, we need to remember to do that.
>
> —1984
>
> *Source:* Ienaga in conversation with Honda Katsuichi (April 20, 1984), in *Taidanshū*, p. 85.

grasp the epoch-making significance of the Constitution of Japan. Minobe's theories construed the Meiji Constitution as constitutionally as possible and tried to realize within its framework the highest possible degree of democracy; paradoxically, his ideas may have been one factor preventing me from understanding the epoch-making significance of the postwar revision of the constitution. At the time I did not know that the original draft of the Constitution of Japan—the so-called MacArthur draft—had been drawn up by the Occupation's General Headquarters; my first contact with the Constitution of Japan was when I read what was published in the newspapers as "the government draft." Popular sovereignty, the renunciation of war, and unconditional guarantees of fundamental human rights were this constitution's fundamental ideals, and as far as they were concerned, far from being opposed, I was in full agreement in principle. Still, I was not deeply moved. I was not moved partly because of my frame of mind at the time, a state I have already described. Furthermore, the constitution renounced war and the means of making war, yet at the time the military was completely disbanded, so I could only take the constitution to be the ratification of what already existed de facto. As for the guarantees of fundamental human rights, the peace preservation laws had already been abolished entirely before the constitution was promulgated, and in fact we enjoyed already a liberty unimaginable in prewar days. That probably explains why I didn't react with deep emotion to the epoch-making significance of the constitution's guarantees of fundamental human rights. My slowness to catch on is a source of embarrassment to me today, but this frame of mind was by no means mine alone.

At the time of the new constitution's promulgation, I felt vaguely uneasy with it and almost felt it was a mistake for the United States to have given the Japanese people democracy and peace. But when it came to the attempt to strip the people of their fundamental human rights and push rearmament on them, I came at last to appreciate the significance of the constitution's peace and democracy. The conservative government formed a military alliance with the United States even after the establishment of the peace treaty, and under the security-treaty system it continued loyally to pursue the anticommunist policies of the Occupation army that dated from the latter half of the Occupation; as it did so, I came to understand acutely the true value of the Constitution of Japan. This was my experience and the common experience, I think, of a good many people. For example, when you look at the *Diary of Takami Jun*,[3] published just recently, the entry for May 3, 1947, is as follows:

> Today is an historic day: the promulgation of the new constitution. It is a political event.
>
> But I have absolutely no interest. Is it only I?
>
> No. For the Japanese intellectual world, it is an "epoch-making phenomenon" in which intellectuals take no interest.
>
> Is it because the constitution has been handed down to us from above? Is it because the constitution was not fought for but given to us?
>
> The previous constitution, too—almost all of Japan's "reforms" were not the result of the people's struggle but were handed down from above. Politics, too, was normally that way.
>
> In Japan politics was normally something handed us. In Japan politics was not something in "close mutual relation

---

3. Takami Jun (1907–1965): writer.

with the spirit," but was in the grasp of one group of politicians. It was practiced with no recognition of, or in opposition
to, the "close mutual relation with the [realm of the] spirit."

And in the entry for October 20, 1947, we find the following
reflections: "Labor dispute at Tōhō [film studio]—settled by the
mass resignation of all the union leaders—crushing defeat. When
the infantile left-wingers went wild, like a second military clique,
I thought we were headed for trouble, but with the reactionary
tide as strong as it is today, I figure I have to support the Communist Party."

In the portion of the diary that follows, there is no explicit
reference to the constitution, but it is clear that the late Takami
Jun faced the changed conditions of the postwar period with a
frame of mind similar to mine. Reading this passage, I realized
once again that my postwar frame of mind was by no means
unique to me.

Some constitutional scholars, much more directly involved
with constitutional issues than Takami, took the same psychological path. The November 15, 1955, issue of the journal *Jurist*
printed the transcript of a symposium entitled "Japan's Judges";
it included the following statements of two judges, Niimura
Yoshihiro and Yokokawa Toshio.

Yokokawa: At the end of the war I myself endured the same
distress as Mr. Niimura did. When the war ended I was 26 or
27, in about my third year as a judge. My contemporaries and
I had not become fully set in our thinking, and in an atmosphere of statism and militarism, to greater or lesser degree
we were not able to remain immune. Looking back now, I'm
embarrassed, but it's a fact. . . . On the other hand, it is a fact
that various things bothered me as a judge. . . . Conditions
were such [during the war] that one could not get by without
dealing to some extent in the black market, yet some people
were indicted for economic crimes because they had dealt in
some slight way in the black market. Naive students were indicted for having violated the peace preservation laws merely
because they read Marx's *Das Kapital* as a group; they were
charged with taking action aimed at changing the national
polity. . . . In these incidents for the most part we could sus-
pend punishment, but we couldn't find the accused not guilty.

To the extent we were true to law and precedent, we had to find them guilty. Each time I came up against such cases, my heart grew heavy, and I was tormented by fundamental questions: what is law? what in the world are judges supposed to do? . . . Having traveled this psychological path, I greeted the day of defeat, and when I thought of the state's path ahead, of our own future, I was quite gloomy. I was utterly unable to acclimate myself to the atmosphere at the end of the war: in particular, that good people got purged along with the bad; that rights and freedom got asserted without limit; that in place of people toadying to the military, people toadied to the Occupation army; that those who till yesterday waved the banner of militarism lacked integrity and now nonchalantly waved the banner of democracy.

In the midst of all this, the new constitution was promulgated, and I had the feeling that this constitution too was based on the ideas of extreme liberalism, nineteenth century liberalism; I didn't take to it immediately. . . . I felt strongly that I wanted to take a leave from the bench and sit by myself in quiet contemplation in order to review the past and prepare for the future. But for various reasons I vacillated, and that never happened. I really do feel embarrassed. But just recently, in particular as the revision of the new constitution has come to be discussed openly, I feel I have come to appreciate fully its virtues. And now—fine technical points aside—I feel strongly that we must defend to the utmost the fundamental spirit of this constitution. . . .

Niimura: I agree. Many people think that in losing the war Japan lost a very great many things. That is true; it is impossible to calculate the sacrifices the people made. But even after subtracting all those sacrifices, I think that the constitution is a net gain. A judge who upholds this constitution: when I think of it that way, I hope to remain a judge for a long time, and I resolve anew to study hard and do a good job.

I have quoted the statements of these two at length, for they are words that apply to my own frame of mind—in particular, the passage in Judge Yokokawa's statement. He had been unable to cotton to the "value" of the Constitution of Japan in the period immediately after its promulgation; now he has "come to appreciate [it] fully . . . in particular, as the revision of the new constitution has come to be discussed openly." Here, too, I learned that I was not the only person to travel the psychological path I did, and, speaking frankly, I was reassured.

Be that as it may, despite the constitution, national policy began to swing back in the direction of militarization and of tightening up the peace preservation laws, and the intellectual world, too, began to turn to the right. And I finally came to the conclusion that I had to discard the passive attitude of my immediate postwar years and come to grips actively with problems of state and society. What precipitated this change was that I came to feel in my bones that with the beginning of the "reverse course," the hard-won guarantees of peace and liberty were in danger of being lost once more. But I must note, too, a precondition for this development: I personally had undergone changes that transformed my whole being.

First among them was an issue concerning my family. I had lived alone until the age of thirty-one, so domestically I had needed to think only of myself; but in November 1944 I had married, and from that point on I had to face head-on issues of the family system. Through personal experience I had come to know full well that this issue involved very difficult contradictions not soluble by any simple means. Much of this touches on the privacy of people close to me, so I shall refrain from speaking here about specifics. However, simply to relate the result, I decided that these problems ought to be solved in conformity with the fundamental ideals of the reform of the family system that was a major fruit of the reforms of postwar democratization. In order to manifest that conviction, I could no longer adhere to the attitude toward others I had lived by until then, virtually without friction; if I was to put my beliefs into practice, I had to resolve not to avoid a fight when a fight was unavoidable. This change in ways of doing things, born of the issues of family relations, was one factor in my undergoing a virtual remodeling. It even led to my taking a stand on the democratization of the workplace, the second most important environment after my family.

As mentioned earlier, I began teaching at the Ōtsuka campus in 1944 as professor at Tokyo Higher Normal School. But after the war the reform of the school system was carried out. When Tokyo University of Education opened for business as a new-style university, violent disputes arose among the old-style higher schools that were its parents. Both Tokyo Humanities and Science Univer-

---

My first serious scholarly look into the field of women's history in the realm of daily life was the study, from an intellectual-historical point of view, of the history of Western clothing for women in Japan. My younger years coincided with the era in which Japanese women began to wear Western clothing, and I witnessed myself, growing up, how women made progress in the wearing of Western clothing even in the face of social criticism and ridicule. . . . [I was sympathetic to new approaches because] in one aspect of my being, I myself was half-academic (not anti-academic) not entirely engrossed in academic history.*

—*Essay, 1985*

Source: Ienaga, "Nihon joseishi," in Ienaga Saburō shū, vol. 16, p. 249.

*In this context "academic" is strongly pejorative; in Japanese half (*han*) and anti (*han*) sound the same, making possible this play on words.

---

sity and Tokyo Higher Normal School, to which I belonged, were located in Ōtsuka; sharp conflicts of opinion arose between them on such matters as the new name and the procedures for setting up the new university, and chaos continued. To me, this was merely a struggle for leadership between the two schools, and I regarded it as a relatively meaningless struggle. So as a member of the faculty, I took the attitude of a bystander and did not get sucked into the whirlpool. In retrospect, it appears that my perception was pretty accurate. In fact, the correct interpretation is that it was a collision between the defensive posture of Tokyo Humanities and Sciences University, seeking to preserve at all costs its special privileges as an old-style university, and the expansionist stance of the Higher Normal School side, demanding a share of the special privileges that Tokyo Humanities and Science University had monopolized. I was indeed smart not to get caught up in the struggle.

   Noticing that I was not leading the Higher Normal side, people on the Humanities and Science side seem to have thought that I favored their side. In the end, the struggle was settled along the lines of a proposal of President Shibanuma Choku, newly appointed by the Ministry of Education: the university was to be managed by a university deliberative council constituted so that the Humanities and Science side held the majority. Under this arrangement, the new university opened its doors, and personnel matters proceeded as the Humanities and Science side intended. The deans of the new Faculty of Letters, the new Faculty of Education, and the new Faculty of Science were all Humanities and Science professors, and all personnel matters were under the control of the university council. According to the schedule set up by this university council, I was transferred right off to be professor at the new university. Not only that, but despite the fact that I was the youngest of the professors of the Faculty of Letters, Dean Fukuhara Rintarō assigned me the post of chair of the history department—on his own and without consultation. It soon became clear that this irregular personnel action was a ploy of the Humanities and Science side to use me as a figurehead. By that, I mean that while I held the important post of chair of the history department, one strange thing after another in history department personnel issues took place, all unbeknownst to me.

The first time I noticed this, the issue was a successor for a professor who was retiring. As I have mentioned, at that time in the new university, faculty councils had not been established, and power over personnel matters in the new university was entirely in the grasp of the university-wide deliberative council. But in the old Humanities and Science University, there was still a faculty council, and that faculty council continued to exercise control over personnel matters for Humanities and Science. So the Humanities and Science faculty council, I learned, planned first to recruit a successor from another university, to appoint him to Humanities and Science, and then slide him over into the new Faculty of Letters. I could not but be indignant. Such an arrangement attempted to import the special privileges of the old university unchanged into the new university, a distinct organization. Confronted with an illegal procedure whereby the successor to a retiree was chosen while the department chair was kept in the dark, I could not stay silent. I lodged a strong protest with Dean Fukuhara, and Fukuhara, who was contemptuous of me, seemed very surprised and made various excuses. But his defense that the retiree had been a Humanities and Science person, so Humanities and Science could decide on his successor, left me open-mouthed in astonishment.

The root of the problem, I saw, was that the faculty councils that were supposed to be established as a matter of course in the new university had not been established; therein lay the source of the disregard for the principles of university self-government—that in defiance of the stipulations of the law, the university-wide deliberative council that had no writ in personnel matters made personnel decisions. So I resolved that a faculty council for the Faculty of Literature simply had to be established and launched a movement for its establishment. But the dean and others desired at all costs to maintain the special privileges of the old university and did not accede to that demand. Not only that, but the likes of President Shibanuma argued that new universities were under the management of a special council of inquiry on the establishment of universities and that none of the other universities had faculty councils. If I thought these were lies, I should ask anyone I cared to—Professor Wagatsuma, who had been chair of the committee that drafted the law of university administration, or anyone else. The dean was talking through his hat.

In order to disprove the dean's assertion, I paid a call out of the blue—in retrospect, I think I acted rashly—on Yanaihara Tadao, dean of the Faculty of General Studies at Tokyo University, and asked him how personnel matters were handled in the Faculty of General Studies, a new faculty that had recently been set up at Tokyo University. In addition, I took depositions from those in charge—at Tokyo University's Faculty of Education, at Ochanomizu Women's University, at Tokyo University of Commerce—on whether personnel matters in new universities were

---

A report of May 1964 in Ningen no kagaku presented the results of a 1948–1954 survey of sexual behavior, and I read that in the sex act in Japan the male was on top 84.5 percent of the time, but that in the United States the female was on top 37.1 percent of the time (the highest frequency) and the male was on top only 10.6 percent of the time (fourth highest). . . . I have to think these figures indicate differences in the socio-historical conditions of the two countries.

—Essay, 1985

Source: Ienaga, "Nihon joseishi to no meguriai," Rekishigaku kenkyū 541 (June 1985); in Ienaga Saburō shū, vol. 16, p. 247.

conducted by faculty councils, and I succeeded in gathering proof that what Dean Fukuhara had said was complete bunk. Based on this, I then presented a proposal to the provisional faculty council of the Faculty of Letters, a body that had been set up at the time as a consultative organ for the dean. (The provisional faculty council had been set up before the legitimate faculty council was set up, in order to solicit the general opinions of the faculty of the new university, but it had neither power over personnel nor authority over the dean and was a complete fraud.) The proposal called for the immediate establishment of a new faculty council. The provisional faculty council adopted this proposal and established a committee to produce a position paper on the subject. I was chosen a member and drafted the request to the university-wide council that a new faculty council be established. After the committee approved it, I submitted it to Dean Fukuhara. But without submitting it to the provisional council for its deliberation, the dean rejected it, writing to me as representative of the committee that we were being too literal-minded, that he wanted us to rethink it.

I was most unhappy, but I reconvened the committee, and we debated it. As a result it was decided that because it was the dean who transmitted the proposal to the council, it would not do to disregard the dean's opinion. Rewriting it in slightly more moderate language, we submitted it again. The dean not only didn't print the request up and distribute it ahead of time to the provisional council, he finally hushed up this request for the establishment of a faculty council. This happened in 1952, and the next year in March, a proposal was presented once again to the provisional faculty council calling for the establishment of a faculty council. This time it passed by an overwhelming majority, 30 to 2. Knowing what was going on in the provisional faculty council of the Faculty of Letters, President Shibanuma and those of his ilk anticipated it by having the university-wide council decide on the establishment of faculty councils. At long last, in April 1952, the faculty council of the Faculty of Letters was established formally.

According to the law, faculty personnel matters had to be handled by a faculty council, so it was clearly illegal for the university-wide council to act in its stead. The astonishing fact is that this illegal activity continued for three years after the opening of Tokyo University of Education; it was due in part to the fact that we were uninformed on legal issues and so in the beginning accepted what the dean said without the slightest doubt. These events made me recognize anew the ironclad rule that rights must be fought for, must be won. They brought home to me the fact that in order to actualize what is right, you need a thorough knowledge of law.

It was just at this time that the police reserve corps, inaugurated by directive of the Occupation army, gradually took shape, and the rearmament of Japan moved forward. The constitution expressly prohibited the maintenance of land, sea, air, and other forces; in the face of this express provision, how could these land, sea, and air forces exist? Herein lay beyond doubt a willful and distorted interpretation of the laws by those in power. In exactly the same way, the regulations stated that faculty councils had to be set up, yet the twisting of the law by President Shibanuma and the others to mean that new universities didn't have faculty councils took advantage of our lack of legal knowledge, and they prevailed for three years. Of course, there were differences in scale—in the one case, Japan; in the other, a single national university. But these two events were a matched pair in twisting the law and its regulations to mean precisely the opposite of what they stated and in attempting to fabricate illegal faits accomplis to suit the desires of those in power. They made me feel acutely the importance of legal interpretation; they also made me think with great urgency that in order for us to bring about democracy, the pressing need was to take back into the hands of the people the laws that had become a weapon of control of those in power. First the home, second the workplace: actual experience in these two stages gradually transformed me, and thus I came at last to tackle on the national scale the destruction of the legal that the progress of rearmament brought about. (In that rearmament took place at the insistence of the United States, the scale involved was indeed world-historical.) And so at long last my eyes were opened politically. Starting not from conceptual knowledge gained from books but from actual problems in matters closest to me personally, I moved for the first time beyond my long-standing ignorance of politics.

Changes in me, demanded unavoidably in my personal world, were one precondition for the practical actions I took beginning about 1952 and 1953. There was also another important

> Because the fifteen-year war was an unrighteous, reckless war begun with unjust and improper goals and means by the Japanese state, and because starting the war and refusing to end the war in timely fashion were both illegal and improper acts of the state, those who died on account of this war—those who stepped forward burning with loyalty and offered their lives, those who did not want to die in this sort of war, who despised war and opposed war yet were driven to their deaths against their will, all those who were caught up willy-nilly in the maelstrom of war and, having no escape, died—all of them alike we should treat as victims of the war. That only some receive veneration, decoration, special treatment, that some are merely honored with memorials, that some are disregarded and forgotten: we should end immediately all such distinctions.
>
> —1979
>
> Source: Ienaga, "Jūgonen sensō ni yoru shi o dō kangaeru ka," *Rekishi tokuhon* (expanded issue, March 1979); in *Ienaga Saburō shū*, vol. 12, p. 260.

element: the freedom of expression in the postwar world that showed me in broad sweep and naked detail actual conditions in all their facets—past and present, society and history and ideas. Before the defeat I had had no way of knowing about these conditions. After the war, even a slow-witted person like me was given the opportunity to broaden his field of vision beyond compare. Japanese history was a field with a particularly large number of taboos, and with the postwar demolition of these taboos, it advanced by leaps and bounds; it is impossible to measure how much rich new knowledge I, a specialist in the study of Japanese history, gained from the new scholarship. For example, many of the secret records of the senior advisers and the military were published, exposing to the light of day what went on in the palace, the cabinet, and the core military group. Up until then, these workings had been veiled in complete secrecy from the people. It became possible to know in vivid detail what activities the military and other Japanese officials had carried out in areas under Japanese control—Korea, "Manchukuo," China proper, Southeast Asia. Information became available for the first time about such things as the existence outside Harbin of Unit 731, the horrendous squad that conducted itself bestially over many years, using several thousand captured foreigners as guinea pigs in live experiments in germ warfare—no less atrocious than Nazi Germany's Auschwitz concentration camp. On the other hand, through the uncovering of vast quantities of censored materials and the like that the prewar authorities had consigned to oblivion, we came also to understand in great detail that there was in Japanese history a proud tradition of resistance to war and of struggle against oppression; many valuable achievements of hitherto virtually unknown "forgotten thinkers" were added to our intellectual heritage. That those contemplating the abolition of the emperor system included not only communists but also liberals and many anonymous ordinary citizens: this, too, was knowledge we couldn't have had except after the war. Before, people refrained even from mentioning the origins of the Ise Shrine; now they published essays on that topic. Before, merely to own the classics of Marxism, beginning with the *Communist Manifesto,* was to put your life in danger, but now we could read them freely, with not a single word deleted. The past and present of ideas and facts relating to gender and the family system, to movements of conflict between classes and against war and against the establishment, to the emperor system and other problems of the fundamental structure of society: under the prewar peace preservation laws it had been impossible in many cases even to study the historical materials, not to mention publish your research. Now we could absorb knowledge about these things freely. Amid such epoch-making changes, my poor narrow horizons expanded enormously, and I adopted ways of thinking unthinkable earlier. There can be no doubt that without these developments, my social awakening would not have taken place. In this sense my remodeling of myself can be said to have its ultimate origin in the freedoms guaranteed by the Constitution of Japan. For that very reason it became unavoidable that I bend my full energies to the protection of those freedoms.

9

TO THE FILING OF THE TEXTBOOK LAWSUITS

B eginning in the mid-1950s, I joined the fight to defend the peace and democracy of the Constitution of Japan, and in the previous chapter I described the route I took. The government had set up a Constitutional Study Committee to lay the ground-work for the revision of the constitution. In opposition to that committee, a study group on constitutional issues was planned to study constitutional problems from the standpoint of scholars and intellectuals. It was organized on June 8, 1958, at the initia-tive of Ōuchi Hyōe, Wagatsuma Sakae, and Miyazawa Toshi-yoshi;[1] I was invited to participate and did so. In existence now for ten years, this study group has persevered in its serious re-search. Nearly every month we hold a regular meeting, and it is our rule that at each meeting a member reports on his research. Sometimes we invite someone who is not a member to give a guest lecture. Not only that, but when important constitutional issues like the revision of the security alliance arise, we either convene an open meeting or issue a declaration, thus proclaiming to society at large the united sense of the members. Moreover, to underline our opposition to the fact that the government ended all celebration of Constitution Day, we have made it a custom to sponsor a public meeting every year on May 3 to commemorate Constitution Day. At these meetings members give lectures, and I, too, have taken my turn.

The progress of rearmament and of plans to revise the consti-tution had the paradoxical effect of heightening popular interest

---

1. Ōuchi Hyōe (1888–1980): economist. Wagatsuma Sakae (1897–1973) and Miyazawa Toshiyoshi (1899–1976): legal scholars.

151

Under the constitution's "land, sea, and air forces . . . will never be maintained" [Article 9], it's strange that there are Self Defense Forces at all—
and dispatching them overseas? That's out of the question. Despite the
fact that this hollowing out of the constitution proceeds apace, not that
many people react sharply against it.

—1990

Source: Interview with Sawachi Hisae (December 20, 1990), Taidanshū, p. 91.

in constitutional issues. Until now I have spoken only of the process whereby I myself came to be interested in constitutional issues, but the development of my awareness of the constitution is
only one example of this nationwide phenomenon. Awareness of
the constitution has grown both broad and deep.

In 1960, as this general trend was taking place, there arose
the struggle over the security treaty, the mass movement in opposition to the Kishi Cabinet's action in ramming through the security treaty between the United States and Japan. This event deserves to be called the development of Japanese democracy to its
broadest. I was involved in this historic event, but my involvement was restricted to a very narrow realm, and it does not merit
particular mention here. I lent more of my energies to issues that
involved my postwar awareness of democracy and were closer to
home for me: democratization of the workplace and the struggle
against the "reform" of history education.

I have already described how the Faculty of Letters of Tokyo
University of Education succeeded in establishing a new faculty
council. Taking the opportunity of the summer of 1954 and the
forced resignation of Dean Fukuhara, the like-minded within that
faculty joined forces and set their hand to reforms aimed at democratizing the faculty and the university. For example, we
pushed through thorough-going reforms, rarely found in other
universities, that made the powers of professors, assistant professors, and lecturers completely equal, at least insofar as the administration of the faculty was concerned. The previous regulation
held that faculty personnel decisions were to be handled only by
the faculty council, of which only full professors were members.
We changed that to a system whereby each faculty decided the

makeup of its council for itself, and in the Faculty of Letters everyone—full professors, assistant professors, lecturers—took part in the entire agenda of the faculty council, including personnel decisions. Moreover, it had been the custom that only professors could be in charge of instruction in a given area. We not only changed that from an individual to a committee task but also made professors, assistant professors, and full-time lecturers eligible. In the Japanese history division to which I belonged, we put striking reforms into effect. We established special division regulations and set up a division council of which all faculty—including even teaching associates—were members, and everything relating to the management of the division had to pass the division council, so that even teaching associates participated in division personnel matters. The Faculty of Letters operated by these procedures to its dying day. At the prompting of the Faculty of Letters, reforms of the system were carried out concerning relations with students, too. We revised the common code of conduct for students, which had been drawn up under the Occupation, apparently with the chief aim of stifling the student movement, and we changed from a permit system to a notification system for student meetings, the organization of student groups, signs, and the like. In addition, we were scrupulous in carrying out policies intended to give all possible weight to the autonomy of students and to achieve good understanding between faculty and students.

This entire range of measures democratizing the university went forward between late 1953 and about 1957. Between 1962 and 1964, the Ikeda Cabinet planned a University Administration Law that would reduce university self-government. At Tokyo University of Education, under a proposal of President Tomonaga Shinichirō,[2] we set up a committee to study the university system and formulate a unified response to the proposed reforms. On

> All people shall have the right to receive an equal education correspondent to their ability, as provided by law.
> —Article 26.1, Constitution of Japan

---

2. Tomonaga Shinichirō (1906–1979): quantum physicist.

June 21, 1964, the university council passed a resolution based on that proposal and stipulating these extremely democratic rules for running the university: the recognition of the university's right to self-government in personnel matters concerning presidents, deans, and faculty; the designation of the faculty councils as the basic locus of university management, with the university council as the body reconciling the interests of the various faculties; and the clarification of the legislative powers of university council and faculty councils (thus setting limits to the autocracy of presidents and deans). With these principles as a basis, we consulted with the Council of National Universities and other groups.

These activities moved ahead with the cooperation of a very large number of people who sought to preserve the self-government and the democratic management of the university. As one of them, I, too, contributed my mite, taking a good deal of time and energy from my scholarship to devote to the democratization of the workplace. Without that experience, I probably wouldn't have been able to write *The History of University Self-Rule*.

Along with the democratization of the workplace, I came to confront head-on a second issue: the "reform" of history education. I have mentioned my participation in the movements aiming to cope with the reactionary educational policies that in the early 1950s were already rising to prominence. The issue on which I have appealed to the public with special urgency was textbook certification. Immediately after the defeat, the publisher Fuzambō asked me to write a general history of Japan, intended eventually for certification for use in junior high school. However, in the early going, the Occupation army adopted a policy of using textbooks written by the Ministry of Education—for junior high school it came to use *The History of Japan*, a book compiled as a companion text to *The Progress of the Country*. So my manuscript could not be a textbook. Thereupon, Fuzambō changed it to a general trade book and published the first edition in April 1947 under the title *New History of Japan*. It sold for what was then a stunningly high price; it was, I think, the first general history written by one person to come out after the defeat.

Thereafter, the publisher Sanseidō entrusted to me the writing of a high-school textbook, and it was at this point that I first experienced the reality of textbook certification. This manuscript underwent certification in 1953. The year 1953 belonged to the

> *[T]he certified textbooks are every last one very similar, with only slight differences in style—meaningless. Textbooks with individuality are multi-dimensional; they are pluralistic; a pluralism must permeate them that allows teachers in the classroom to select what is most suitable for their own use.*
>
> *So I tried to make these things [women's history, family life] character-istics of my text, something that the other textbooks didn't have; at the same time, believing that it is important in public education to make peo-ple grasp historically that . . . family life was changed fundamentally in the postwar era, amid such wholesale changes as the sections of the civil law on the family and inheritance: these things I added and made characteris-tics of my text.*
>
> *—Court testimony, 1969*
>
> *Source:* Statement under direct examination, July 12, 1969; in Ienaga, *Shōgen-shū,* p. 126.

era of the reverse course, but so far as concerns textbook certifi-cation, 1953 was the doldrums—I never heard of problems arising on this account. It was a time of the doldrums, yet in my first brush with the certification process, my manuscript was declared unacceptable for astonishing reasons. The following will give a general idea of what was communicated to me as the rationale for its "unacceptable" rating:

- my explanation of the family system in the Tokugawa era was filled with malice toward the Japanese family system;
- my treatment of peasant uprisings seemed to legitimize il-legal activity;
- I devoted many pages to historical facts about the Pacific War and the postwar era, but these were things the pupils had all experienced, so it would be better to delete them all.

It was astonishing.

At the time, the Ministry of Education still had no full-time certifiers of textbooks, and it conducted reviews by setting up five-person committees of specialists and teachers to review given manuscripts. One member of the committee happened to give me very bad marks on grounds like those I just cited, so my manuscript did not pass. But under the system in force at the time, I could submit the same manuscript once more, to be examined by a committee made up of different people. So I resubmitted the manuscript without changing a single word. This time it passed certification virtually unchanged, so I suffered no actual damage. But my very first contact with textbook certification made me acutely aware that it posed serious problems. Thereafter, in August 1955 the Minshūtō[3] published a pamphlet entitled "Alarming Textbook Problems." Naming several civics texts, it slandered them as biased. That brought the textbook issue to the fore for the public at large.

The second set of two education laws was submitted to the Diet in 1956. The first law concerned the administration of local education and proposed to change from elected school committees to appointed school committees. The second law proposed to "strengthen" the certification of textbooks. In opposition, the same kind of violent anti-movement boiled up that had greeted the first set of two education laws, but in the end the law to end the election of school committees passed the Diet and became one major step in the reactionary trend in the elementary, junior high, and high schools. But fortunately the violent anti-movement succeeded against the proposal concerning textbook certification, and the law died stillborn. Nevertheless, by budgetary act the government established a full-time textbook inspectorate and increased the number of members of its textbook certification consultative committees, thereby paving the way for the "strengthening" of the certification system. Since then, textbook certification has become "stronger" with each passing year. Paralleling these developments, the "reform" of the code of ethics for teachers also moved forward, and the code of ethics for teachers of 1951, which emphasized the spirit of science and democracy and peace, became worse with each revision. That development, too, functioned as a stimulus to the gradual "strengthening" of textbook certification.

In these circumstances I submitted manuscripts for certification twice, in 1955 and 1957. In 1955 I received conditional certification—many on the committee suggested a large number of

---

3. Minshūtō (1947–1950): Democratic Party.

revisions. For my part, I had to decide whether to accept the suggestions. If I did not accept them, I had to submit to the Ministry of Education an explanation stating clearly why I did not.

Among these suggested revisions were the following:

- An illustration entitled "Women and children of Hiroshima, injured by the atomic bomb, running this way and that trying to escape" should be deleted.
- "The judgment that the existence of the House of Peers and the Privy Council hindered the development of democracy is not appropriate. Isn't it the case that the existence of these two bodies blocked high-handed behavior on the part of the political parties?"
- In reaction to the passage governing an illustration, "Relatives of soldiers who died in the Sino-Japanese war," which read, "It would not do to forget, in view of the sparkling victory, that bitter sacrifices were involved": "At least get rid of the text."
- In response to my text that "the Japanese army occupied Beijing, Nanjing, Hangzhou, Guangdong, one after the other, and spread the fighting to all of China": "Correct 'spread the fighting to all of China.' "
- In response to my "Even the clothing—for the boys, military caps and gaiters, for the girls, cotton bloomers—was painted over in wartime colors": "As to the expression 'painted over in wartime colors,' preferences aside, wasn't that attire the most convenient?"

Most of the opinions were as astonishing as these and entirely disregarded peace and democracy.

Fortunately, at the moment I had some spare time. I rejected as many of the proposed changes as possible; in cases where I could express the same meaning merely by changing a few words, I did so. Hence the damage was not so great, and somehow I continued to win certification. Still, unlike my experience in 1952, I was unable to avoid damage entirely.

At the time of the 1957 certification, full-time certifiers were already in place, and certification was one notch "stronger." Acceding to a request from a federation of those of us hoping to write civics texts, the Ministry had agreed in cases of noncertification to issue its reasons in writing. My text failed two times running. The first time, this was the statement of reasons:

> This manuscript is idiosyncratic in its structure, narrative, and expressions, and as a text in Japanese history for high school civics, it has the following shortcomings:
>
> First, in not a few cases it lacks soundness in its selection of facts. That is to say, in Japanese history, one requires (Certification Criteria: Absolutely Necessary Condition 3.3.1) that "at all times one emphasize concrete historical facts and, based on positivist, objective methods, one cultivate the ability and the desire to understand the development of Japanese history scientifically." But this manuscript lacks soundness in its selection of facts, especially in section 4 of Part IV. . . .
>
> Second, the narrative often runs to editorializing, and in places words and tone are not appropriate to a textbook.
>
> Third, because of excessive fervor to encourage soul-searching rather than interest in historical accuracy about the past, there is a profound sense in which it veers from the goals of teaching Japanese history: "through academic activities to recognize the efforts of ancestors, to heighten one's consciousness of being Japanese, to instill a rich love of the race."
>
> For these reasons, this manuscript as a whole cannot be considered appropriate as a text for Japanese history in high school civics instruction.

This statement of reasons for noncertification itself is a shocking document. In the first place, consider "encourage soul-searching rather than interest in historical accuracy about the past." The Constitution of Japan and the Fundamental Law of Education [1947] are based on deep soul-searching about the war and grew out of the intent that such a calamity not happen again.

Education shall aim at the full development of personality, striving for the rearing of the people, sound in mind and body, who shall love truth and justice, esteem individual value, respect labor and have a deep sense of responsibility, and be imbued with the independent spirit, as builders of a peaceful state and society.

—Article I, Fundamental Law of Education

In this sense soul-searching is something that a civics text must emphasize, yet here it is given as a reason for withholding certification—surely, extreme disregard of the constitution! The rejection is clearly illegal. At the time I was already thinking about going to court in order to establish the unconstitutionality and illegality of certification, and I consulted privately with friends who had received rejections for similar reasons. But the time wasn't yet ripe, and in the end we didn't act. Having no alternative, I rewrote several parts of the manuscript and resubmitted it, and it was turned down again. The third time it just barely passed muster. As with the previous time, this certification did not damage the manuscript so severely as to distort my fundamental assertions. Still, the manuscript did not escape without considerable damage. Thereafter, certification became more and more severe, and in 1960, the certification of primary-school civics texts even became the subject of debate in the Diet. Day by day, certification clearly was moving in a lamentable direction. But for several years my own texts did not have to undergo certification, and I did not experience for myself the actual state of certification as it existed then, so I won't go into that here.

In 1960 the code of ethics for high school teachers was revised completely, and textbooks had to be revised to match those changes. The new code of ethics for teachers of Japanese history showed startling traces of "reform," and it was not a happy task to rewrite to suit it, but I had no choice. So I tried to create the very best text possible within the framework of the code of ethics and submitted the revised manuscript in 1962. In April 1963, after the manuscript had sat for six months, I received notice that my manuscript had not been certified. The reasons this time were not, as in 1957, reasonably specific. (Even the 1957 reasons, while specific, contained many nonspecific and abstract criticisms, such as "not a few places in which the selection of facts is not appropriate" or "narration runs to editorializing.") There was only one line: "This manuscript is seriously deficient in accuracy and choice of contents." This gave us no way of knowing what parts did not meet certification, so the publishers and I set off to the Ministry and heard from the person responsible for certification an oral statement of passages that counted in the reasons for rejection. Every one of them was a shocker. For example, in the section on the Pacific War there were war photographs—"Air assault on Japan," "The atomic bomb and Hiroshima, turned into a wasteland by the bomb," "Wartime social customs." Pointing to these, the man said, "The manuscript includes gloomy photographs of war." Pointing next to two photographs—"Students heading off for the army" and "Schoolgirls working in a factory"—he said, "Here the positive side emerges showing that the people cooperated for all they were worth in the war, but on the following page there is a photograph that shows 'ravages of war.' The overall picture is too negative." This treatment of the war, he said, was one reason for rejection. The photograph of "ravages of war" showed a one-armed veteran begging on a street corner. Accompanying it was this text: "Even after the war ended, the limbs that soldiers lost never came back. This grim figure warns us in eloquent fashion of the important meaning of one passage in the preamble to the constitution: 'determined . . . that never again shall we be visited with the horrors of war through the action of government.'" I included this photograph after considering its educational purpose, to try to help students understand the spirit of the constitution, yet it was made a reason for rejection. The other reasons I was given then were all pretty much like these—in light of the spirit of the constitution and the Fundamental Law of Education, completely upside-down. Several careless mistakes were pointed out, but they could be corrected easily, so they can't have been reasons for rejection.

These reasons for rejection left me utterly unpersuaded. I could give up and yield the field to textbooks that were even less desirable, or I could keep trying under the existing certification system to produce a textbook with a bit more conscience than the others. I chose the latter course, thinking I might somehow serve the cause of holding off—if only slightly—the complete degradation of textbooks. So with reluctance I rewrote several passages and resubmitted the manuscript. This second submission sat for a very long time and then, in late March 1964, received certification with conditions attached; I was notified orally of some three hundred passages where revision was desired. The passages that were particularly troublesome among these requests for revision were "B" items—on the surface, I didn't absolutely have to revise them. Still, the Ministry tenaciously repeated its requests for revisions of the passages it didn't like. When it finally came to April 20, the deadline for that year's textbook catalog, the Ministry

Photo 9.1   The photograph at issue in 1963. Photo courtesy of the National League for Support of the School Textbook Screening Suit.

listed its final requests for revision, including a new revised opinion, and I was backed into a corner. Unless I met them, I wouldn't be able to exhibit the book in that year's textbook fair.

I was in an absolute bind, having to choose one of two very unhappy courses of action: either give up and throw the manuscript away, or respond dishonestly to illegal requests and give the pupils a text that to the extent possible included my meaning and choose another arena to contest illegal certification. It was most mortifying. But after thinking things over, I chose the latter and in fact got the text certified. Yet this time, unlike earlier, my manuscript really did get butchered. In the end I had to excise several important passages. For example, "The tales of 'the age of the gods,' of course, but also the passages about the first several emperors beginning with Emperor Jimmu, were all thought up after the Imperial House had unified Japan in order to legitimate the Imperial House's rule over Japan." And "The refusal of Uchimura Kanzō, a Christian, to bow to the Imperial Rescript on Education was rejected as blasphemous, and he lost his position as teacher at First Higher School."[4] And illustrations, too: I had to delete a photograph entitled "People who oppose rearmament" of a demonstration with people carrying signs saying, "Defend the peace constitution." Most of these passages had been included in the 1956 edition that had been certified and in the 1962 edition that had been 25 percent revised, and for many years they had been used in the schools without problem. So it seems safe to say it was a completely arbitrary misuse of power to force deletions on me now. As I faced the final coercion on April 20, I thought I could not swallow changes that went any further. I felt that the time had come to begin the court battle I had long contemplated.

But in order to fight the issue in the courts, I needed the cooperation of legal experts. In the first place, I couldn't proceed with a suit without a lawyer who would take on the job, and it was highly desirable to obtain the reasoned support of legal scholars. However, in the world of legal scholarship, the study of laws relating to education was the most backward field of all. Indeed, there simply were no specialized legal studies dealing with textbook certification. If specialists in the law wouldn't do it, I had no

---

4. Uchimura Kanzō (1861–1930): Christian essayist, editor, founder of No-Church movement.

choice but to demonstrate the unconstitutionality and illegality of textbook certification myself. So first I set into print painstakingly all the illegal requests for changes in 1963, and at the same time, I began to write *The Certification of Textbooks*. Nihon hyōronsha agreed to publish it, and it appeared in March 1965. Besides pressing on with that task, I consulted with Oyama Hiroshi, a lawyer who had been helpful with earlier "education trials," and asked him to take on my suit.

Here I perhaps need to state in a bit more detail the psychology that led me to think so seriously about fighting textbook certification in court, something that no one had thought seriously about before then. As I related earlier, already in my first year in middle school I had read Minobe's books on constitutional law, and from early on my interest in legal issues was deeper than the average person's. The Meiji Constitution itself did not protect the rights of the people fully, and the peace preservation legislation enacted under it reduced the rights of the people virtually to zero. From my study before the war of Minobe's constitutional theory, I realized that even under such a legal system, knowledgeable people like Minobe might still be able to construct a theory that made the law a shield to defend the rights of the people. But judging from the way the general public at the time accepted the fact that many of their freedoms were taken from them in the name of the law, law was no more than a tool whereby those in power ruled the people. So it was inevitable that we found it difficult to conceive of law as also being a shield to defend the rights of the people.

The communists were the immediate targets of the peace preservation legislation, and they in particular stipulated from the first that judges were class judges, so they came to think of the courts only as places to carry on propaganda for their own ideas and arguments. They had conducted court fights based on that view for some time. In fact, the prewar courts were full of judges who had already decided communists were "traitors," so it was not at all without reason that the communists conceived of the courts only in that way. But the Constitution of Japan guarantees the fundamental human rights of the people as something that can never be infringed, so one might expect that after the war the situation had to change in its very fundamentals. It was not universally the case that postwar courts operated in accord with

> I miscalculated greatly; since the court decisions in the years right after the war were handed down by judges still infused with the spirit of the Meiji Constitution, I thought it unavoidable that their thinking would not be in line with the Constitution of Japan, but that as people educated under the new constitution gradually rose to power, they would hand down judgments appropriate to the spirit of the Constitution of Japan. And I imagined that the people as a whole would also change in the same way; but on the contrary, it's people like us old fogies who cling to the Constitution of Japan and young people are entirely uninterested. It's truly regrettable.
>
> —1994
>
> Source: Ienaga, *Taidanshū*, pp. 175–176. His interlocutor is Takeda Kiyoko.

the ideals of the constitution and the trend toward protecting the rights of the people, but the postwar courts have produced a number of excellent judgments deserving of our admiration. On this point the judgment that most impressed me was the decision the Tokyo District Court handed down on May 11, 1955, in the Tokyo University/Popolo Case. The Popolo Incident at Tokyo University involved the following: on February 20, 1952, a student theater troupe gave a performance in a Tōdai classroom; the troupe had received permission for the performance. During the performance, a Motofuji police officer who had infiltrated in civilian clothes was spotted. The students seized him, took away his official notebook, and, on examining it, exposed the shocking fact that on a virtually daily basis the Motofuji police station carried on spying at Tōdai—everything from the actions of student groups to the moral character of professors.

The Motofuji police arrested a student at the scene and accused him of having violated the law against crimes of violence, and the upshot was the Popolo decision. Taking the police notebook as evidence, the judges recognized that the police had carried on long-term spying against Tōdai and that the officer's presence at the Popolo troupe's performance was one facet of that spying, and it held that the spying constituted illegal action infringing on university self-government. It recognized the measures the students had taken against this illegal activity as acts of legitimate resistance and found the students innocent. lowing passage is from one section of the judgment:

> In view of the concrete meaning of university self-government, we must consider it a matter of course that when the police, under the guise of upholding peace and order, undertake unlimited police activity within the university, the university has a legitimate right to reject this. . . . The legal value of academic freedom and university self-government is too precious to countenance a situation in which, under the unilateral determination on the part of the police of police necessity, all fields of internal university activity are constantly under police observation and investigation. . . . Under the constitution the activity of the Motofuji police in entering the campus places too great a weight on the necessities of police action and overlooks the constitutional demand concerning academic freedom . . . and we must hold that it is illegal activity that exceeds the limits of official competence. . . . Merely to stand by while illegal acts of governmental authorities take place before one's eyes and not to take all appropriate steps to oppose and resist them is to throw away one's own liberty. Liberty is easily infringed upon unless, in the face of attacks on it, one always protects it against damage with a certain defensive posture. That the defendant revealed the illegality of official acts by the authorities and tried to defend his right of freedom, that before seeking relief through legal procedures, he first exposed the illegal acts himself, and that he called to account this activity that appeared to violate his constitutional rights—even if, in the process, accompanying the excitation and arousing of emotions against this illegal activity, he could not avoid falling into mass psychology and added an element of violence to his behavior—at least to the extent that he stayed within the framework recognized in the prior section, his actions themselves must be held to be acts repelling, blocking illegal actions of the authorities, actions infringing upon his liberty.

This judgment not only showed a comprehension of the essence of university self-government that few university professors could match, but in holding that the people must exercise their right of resistance against illegal abuse of power, it had truly epoch-making significance. When, alerted to it by my colleague

Professor I., I read the original text of the judgment, I was over-come with admiration and published an essay explaining the sig-nificance of this judgment on the Op-Ed page of the *Asahi*. My essay, "The People Too Have the Right to Resist—Thoughts on the Judgment in the Police Notebook Incident," was published on June 14, 1954. I believe this essay of mine was the first published critique of the judgment in the Popolo Incident.

Nor was this the only great judgment the courts handed down. In May 1956, in the Maizuru Incident in which Abe Kōzō, professor of Tokyo Metropolitan University, was the accused, the Tokyo District Court handed down a verdict of innocent roughly similar to the judgment in the Popolo Incident. Again, in July of the same year, it handed down a judgment in an incident involv-ing the prohibition on issuance of travel tickets to China; it held the actions of the civil bureau of the Tokyo District Court to have been illegal. And in March 1959 the same Tokyo District Court handed down its bold judgment—the famous Date judgment—in the incident of a disturbance on the Sunakawa Base: that the sta-tioning of the American army was in violation of the constitution. One after the other, these were great decisions that made full use of the independence of the judiciary. Judges with conscience handed down decisions permeated with the ideals of the constitu-tion, one after the other: this fact made me recognize anew the role of the courts, and it greatly encouraged me, for I had long ago begun to think of the positive aspect of law as a shield protecting the rights of the people. The powerful impact of this whole range of good court precedents was one major reason I came to tackle constitutional issues with such fervor.

It would not do, either, to overlook the fact that in the back-ground against which these precedents continued to appear, his-torical conditions were developing that led to the deepening of the popular consciousness of the constitution. As I have already said, the constitution was first established as something bestowed on the people, but in reaction against the activities of the Occupa-tion army and the Japanese government that aimed at destroying it, the constitution gradually became the flesh and blood of the Japanese people. Judges, too, were members of the people and so could not escape being affected decisively by the constitutional consciousness of the people, and as mediators between interested parties in the courts, they also were in a position to be governed

Ienaga's text (one example of 41 passages at issue in 1981 and of the give-and-take between the certifiers and Ienaga): "In China, the Xi'an Incident gave rise to a united front between the Kuomintang government and the Communist Party against Japan and to a firm determination to resist Japan's aggression [*shinryaku*] and recover China's sovereignty."

Certifier's suggested amendment: "This phrase 'Japan's aggression'—it's a matter of usage, but . . . I think that in today's societal circumstances [the certifier mentions the Pact of Paris and the judgment of the Tokyo war crimes trial] the phrase 'aggressive war' has a very strong connotation . . . of criminality; therefore it is a term that in the case of one's own country vis-à-vis another country has a clear value judgment, and I should like to ask you, from an educational point of view, to reconsider its use in your own country's textbook. [Ienaga had used the term 'aggression' of Ethiopia and Poland but the term 'advance' (*shinshutsu*) of the earlier European encroachment on China.] In the case of Japan, too, I should like to request that you use 'advance.' "

Ienaga's response: "Aggression against China is objective fact, and not simply judgment, so I will not change it. 'Military advance' and the like are the same deception as substituting 'change direction' for 'retreat' [the censors did so during the Pacific War] or 'the end of the war' for 'the defeat' [many people did so after August 15, 1945], and in genuine education such deception should not be allowed. True patriotism expresses itself in recognizing frankly one's own country's mistakes and working so that they will not be repeated."

Ministry request in conference to work out differences: " 'Japan's aggression' is a phrase that carries the judgment 'aggression,' so it may be okay for foreign countries to speak of Japan's aggression, but for Japan as subject to speak of aggression? There's no objection if China considers it 'aggression.' . . . [T]he problem is that you use 'advance' to speak of the European countries and 'aggression' only of Japan. There would be no objection if you said here that the Chinese 'attempted to resist Japan's aggression and recover their own sovereignty. . . .' "

Ienaga's second response: "There is no need to use the same word for aggression after the outlawing of war and aggression before then. [Ienaga argues that the Kellogg-Briand Pact of 1928 outlawed war and summons noted legal experts to defend this usage.] To teach 'aggression' as 'aggression' is correct patriotic education; education that hides 'aggression' behind euphemisms and does not exhaust all efforts to prevent the danger that the next generation will again commit mistakes cannot escape the censure that the disastrous wartime education merited."

Final version: approved unchanged. Ienaga noted that this language had appeared before 1950 without objection and had passed certification in 1958 and 1963–1964. He saw the new demands of 1981 as symptomatic of escalation on the part of the Ministry of Education. Not all cases ended with the text unchanged, and regardless of the end result, the process took enormous amounts of the time and energy of Ienaga, the publisher, and Ienaga's support group.

Source: Ienaga, *'Himitsu' kentei no kiroku* (Tokyo: Meicho kankōkai, 1993), pp. 91–94.

in an immediate sense by the renewal of popular awareness of the constitution. As the most straightforward examples of how the deepening of the people's constitutional consciousness moved the courts, I can cite—in addition to the famous precedents in legal interpretation I have already mentioned—a whole range of not-guilty judgments: the Matsukawa Incident, the Yakai Incident, the Sugo Incident, the Sachiura Incident, the Futamata Incident. These cases were court struggles carried forward with the avid interest and support of a broad public, and they succeeded in winning not-guilty verdicts. In particular, in Matsukawa, Yakai, and the other cases, first and second trials both handed down guilty verdicts that included death sentences, producing sacrificial victims who faced death by hanging because of false charges. But on appeal to the Supreme Court they were remanded to the original court and on retrial found innocent. (To be sure, these cases saw all sorts of strange reversals: in the Matsukawa and Sachiura cases, not-guilty verdicts were confirmed on appeal; but in the Yakai Incident, on second appeal, the appeals court threw out the not-guilty verdict, and on second retrial the verdict was guilty once again.) As these cases developed, they demonstrated clearly that you cannot achieve fair trial unless you raise the people's rights consciousness. How was this? In these cases, external critiques of the cases—in the Matsukawa case, Hirotsu Kazuo's *Matsukawa Trial,* in Yakai, Masaki Hiroshi's *Judge* and the movie *Mid-Day Darkness*—struck a broad and deep chord among the people, and warm material and spiritual support offered the lawyers was a major force favorable to the courtroom struggle.[5] For that very reason, those in power characterized external criticism as "static" and exerted themselves to criticize and slander support movements and critiques of the courts.

Beginning about the time of the Popolo Incident, I had come to pay close attention to trends in the Japanese courts, and I could not ignore this criticism and slander, which sought to stifle precisely those voices calling for fair trials that had come to be prominent among the people. Aiming to defend the legitimacy and legality of the trial critiques of Hirotsu and Masaki from a theoretical perspective, I lent my modest talents to the issue, en-

---

5. Hirotsu Kazuo (1891–1968): author, critic. *Mid-Day Darkness* (1956): Imai Tadashi, director, based on Masaki's book.

gaging in debates in such magazines as *Sekai* and *Hōritsu jihō* with
Tanaka Kōtarō, chief justice of the Supreme Court, and Kumagai
Hiromu, judge of the Tokyo District Court, and publishing *Criticism of the Courts* in November 1969.[6] Thus, my interest in court
issues extended even to my research topics as a historian, and in
1972 I published a collection of scholarly essays entitled *A Historical Examination of the Independence of the Judiciary.* This particular
interest of mine in trials lay at the root of my psychology in thinking of court battle as a means to make clear the illegality and inappropriateness of textbook certification.

In the debates about criticism of the courts, however, I had
absolutely no direct connection with the trials themselves. Instead, I merely defended, indirectly and purely theoretically, those
who were actually criticizing the trials. In addition, I began to appear occasionally as a witness in actual trials and gradually built
up experience as a committed participant in actual court cases. I
refer to my involvement in the series of court cases known at large
as the "education trials." Since the enactment of the two education laws, state regulation of the educational world had become
stricter each year. The code of ethics for teachers, which had been
at first merely a useful reference in teaching, became a legal regulation with binding force, and textbook certification was
"strengthened" and in fact came close to government compilation. Direct pressures on teachers increased, too. For example, beginning in 1957 and over the opposition of the teachers' union,
teachers came under more rigorous evaluation. The opposition of
the teachers' union at this time was extremely violent, and the
government arrested and indicted most of the leaders of the opposition movement. Thus, court battles—"education trials"—
took place nationwide between educators trying to defend freedom of education and those in power.

When the Tokyo District Court heard the case of the struggle
of the Tokyo teachers' union against teacher evaluation, the team
of defense lawyers asked several dozen scholars and others involved in education to testify to the historical significance of
teacher evaluation in the context of changes in school administration before and after the war, hoping thereby to establish the le-

6. Tanaka Kōtarō (1890–1974): legal scholar, judge. Kumagai Hiromu (1913–1992): judge.

gitimacy of resistance to teacher evaluation. The record of this broad range of testimony by many witnesses on the history of education was collected in the Iwanami Shinsho volume *Japanese Education: Testimony in the Education Lawsuits*. In essence, the interpretation and application of the laws are not simply a matter of semantic analysis of the language of the laws; they involve the study of the specific historical and social facts that form the background of the laws, those that form their base. From this point of view, jurisprudence and history are in essence close and inseparable. Yet in the past there had been virtually no communication between the two scholarly worlds. A specialty called the history of legal institutions formed the only link between history and jurisprudence, but in fact, scholars of the history of legal institutions paid attention exclusively to the study of ancient law and feudal law and had shown virtually no interest in problems of contemporary law that were common to the history of legal institutions and to jurisprudence.

Thereafter, too, "education trials" were brought one after the other, not merely in relation to struggles in opposition to teacher-competency tests but also to such other disputes as the struggle against lectures by ex-government officials; in particular, they appeared in most condensed form in the fight against nationwide achievement testing. In these education trials, the defendants always sought the testimony of academic witnesses. On the one hand, by testifying from the point of view of legal studies to the illegality of the educational administration that was the cause of the strife, and on the other, by making clear the history of educational administration, we testified to the reactionary role of teacher-competency tests and academic achievement tests, and for the most part, courts came to allow this sort of testimony. Following the Tokyo teachers' union case, I appeared in court as a witness in the case of the Osaka teachers' union's struggle against competency testing and offered testimony about prewar and postwar changes in educational administration. As in the Tokyo teachers' union case, so here, there was no time to divide up the testimony so that twenty or thirty scholars could each testify from personal experience, and I had to give testimony on the whole history of prewar and postwar education. This was a good chance to study once again the historical roots of the education problem.

On May 28, 1963, I took the witness stand in the Osaka

> *What is important in a trial is not necessarily the judgment alone but what the goals of the parties concerned were . . . and what sort of effort they mounted. If that is so, then testimony is enormously important, and the responsibility of the witness is a heavy one. To the extent that the education trials are important in the history of contemporary Japan, the court testimony is of great importance.*
>
> *I have committed myself as witness in many education trials and in addition have repeated experience as plaintiff in my own lawsuits. No matter how a given court case has ended or will end, I have tried on the witness stand to do my very best. . . . Hence I can't help considering my court testimony as work filled with passion, if not better than my written work, at least no worse.*
>
> *—1998*
>
> Source: Ienaga, Shōgenshū, p. 345.

teachers' union case, in the courtroom of the Tokyo District Court borrowed for circuit session. On February 10, 1964, I gave the same testimony before the Takamatsu District Court in a case of struggle against "reform" of the educational curriculum. I took the stand many times in 'education trials,' was exposed to cross-examination, and experienced firsthand the reality of trials. Up until then, I had understood trials only through documents, theoretically, as a third party. My interest in the courts deepened gradually. As these education trials took place one after the other before my very eyes, I could only regret that they were defensive wars only, with those trying to defend correct education indicted by those in power and made to sit in the dock as criminal defendants. Of course, as I had experienced in the certifications of my own textbook, these struggles over education originated in the fact that school administration that ran counter to the ideals of the constitution was being rammed through. Wasn't it necessary now, I thought, to have at least one education trial in which defense and offense changed places and those defending correct education were the plaintiffs? These thoughts gradually took shape, and when finally the textbook certification process became so extreme in its illegality and inappropriateness that I could no longer stomach it, I came to the point of wanting, no matter what the cost, to lodge a suit on the points at issue in the certifications of 1963 and 1964.

My involvement in these education trials was the second motive contributing to my resolve to undertake these new and unprecedented education trials, the textbook trials. Having been involved in the education trials, I had come into contact with very able lawyers who were skilled in this kind of case. In particular, I had asked Counsel Oyama, the most deeply involved, to take my case. After serious study, Oyama and his partners came to the conclusion that this was an unprecedented charge and would present difficulties, but in light of the importance of the issue, they did want very much to carve out new precedent. So gradually the case became a reality. On June 12, 1965, we lodged the complaint with the Tokyo District Court and came to be heard by that court's Petty Bench II (for civil suits).

In passing, I should note that I appeared twice more as a witness in education trials. On December 20, 1965, I went to Hokkaido and appeared in court at the trial of the incidents of protest against academic achievement tests that had arisen in two places, Asahikawa and Utanobori, and offered the same testimony on the history of education as I had in the Osaka teachers' union case and the Takamatsu teachers' union case. Then, on February 16, 1966, I offered the same testimony at the time of the Morioka District Court's circuit session on the Iwate teachers' union struggle against achievement tests. These education trials resulted in various judgments, some good and some bad, but several courts handed down judgments denying the illegality of opposition movements that tried to defend proper education. For example, on April 18, 1962, in the incident of the Tokyo teachers' union fight against evaluation, the Tokyo District Court handed down a verdict of not guilty, as did the Osaka District Court on March 30, 1964, in the case of the Osaka teachers' union fight against academic achievement tests. But these two not-guilty verdicts both reached their not-guilty conclusions purely from an interpretation of labor regulations; the text of the judgments did not even mention issues of education proper. Our testimony concerning the history of education may have had an important influence in shaping the beliefs of the court, but the texts of the judgments do not reflect it. However, the verdict handed down on May 25, 1966, in the incident of the Asahikawa fight against academic achievement testing clearly mentions education proper and states that from that point of view, nationwide academic achievement testing is illegal. This was not the first judgment holding academic achievement tests to be illegal. Already on March 16, 1964, the Kokura branch of the Fukuoka District Court had ruled that way, and there was a somewhat weaker precedent in that direction in a judgment of May 13, 1964, by the Fukuoka Superior Court. But in both cases, regrettably, the findings were relatively abstract and did not prove definitively the illegality of academic achievement tests. At this point, on May 13, 1966, the Osaka District Court handed down its judgment of the illegality of the tests, adducing much more concrete reasons than had the Kokura branch court.

It interpreted Article 10 of the Fundamental Law of Education as a regulation intended to preclude Ministry control of school administration. It even held that in establishing national standards for the high school curriculum, the Ministry of Education should be limited to the number of hours of instruction and the number of basic units, that on matters outside this realm of general principles even the code of ethics for teachers had no legal force. It stated clearly that nationwide academic achievement testing was an illegal activity that used administrative authority to interfere inappropriately in education. In particular, this judgment emphasized that the existing Fundamental Law of Education was promulgated in accordance with the spirit of the constitution and pointed out at the same time that the Fundamental Law had its basis in soul-searching about the uniform national control of education in the prewar era. The judgment contains the following passage:

> Hitherto in Japan education was supervised and controlled by a system of school administration that included state control—specifically, a centralized bureaucratic structure, and this control extended not simply to school administration but to educational content itself. That it distorted Japan's education is prominent historical fact. In Articles 1 and 2 of its Preamble, the Fundamental Law of Education stipulates the goals of education; in Articles 8 and 9 it sets up regulations, respectively, for the political and religious neutrality of education; and in Article 10, school administration, it establishes

the aforementioned regulations. This too cannot be without relation to the above historical facts.

The judgment of the Asahikawa District Court emphasized in even more detail the limits on school administration. It stated that Article 10 of the Fundamental Law of Education

> suppresses state administrative interference in educational content (particularly interference by force) and guarantees the independence of educational activity. Basing itself on the ideal of revering the free, imaginative, independent activity of teachers, it states clearly that the duties of school administration lie in preparing and ensuring the conditions for education to take place.

From this viewpoint it finds academic achievement tests to be illegal and also states clearly that the existing education regulations arose from soul-searching about the history of undemocratic school administration in the prewar era. The judgment states:

> Article 10 of the Fundamental Law of Education has as its title "School Administration" and stipulates, "Education shall not be subject to improper control, but it shall be directly responsible to the whole people. On the basis of this realization, school administration shall aim at the adjustment and establishment of the various conditions required for the pursuit of the aim of education and should be thought of in light of such conditions as this, that that law was based on soul-searching about the strongly centralized, uniform, formal control of education exercised by the Ministers of Education and the Interior and the military in the prewar and wartime eras."

After that comes the interpretation of the same articles I cited earlier. In the case of academic achievement tests before the Osaka District Court, I don't know how the trial proceeded, so I don't understand the basis for the mention of prewar history that appears in the judgment, either. But in Asahikawa District Court I gave lengthy evidence from about 10 A.M. to nearly 3 P.M., testifying to the history of prewar and postwar school administration. So I think we can say that the judgment clearly accepts my testimony. It gives me great pleasure that my trip to Asahikawa in the depths of winter to take the witness stand was not in vain.

10

THE TEXTBOOK TRIALS AND THE STRUGGLE AT TOKYO UNIVERSITY OF EDUCATION

Lodging the unprecedented suit charging that textbook certification was illegal was entirely my idea. The legal scholars, the teachers' unions, the publication workers, the authors of textbooks who by then had come to oppose government control of education—none of them had thought of it. On the contrary, discouraging voices even suggested that there was no hope of success, so it would be better to give up. For me, however, victory or defeat in the courts was a secondary concern. Even if I could not win final victory, I thought there was significance enough in simply fighting it out in the courts. After serious study, Counsel Oyama Hiroshi had taken on the task of representing me together with Counsels Arai Akira and Imanaga Hiroaki, and on June 12, 1965, we lodged the suit in Tokyo District Court. So began the constitutional trial of the century; it has lasted now for twelve long years.

I had encountered contrary advice, yet with full awareness of the risks I decided on the suit. Why? In addition to the background I described in the last chapter, my frame of mind was as follows. Up to the defeat in 1945, the Japanese people received a uniform education from their textbooks, and in accordance with government policy, that education was permeated by an unscientific, undemocratic, and bellicose spirit. Before the war, via education in the schools and most notably through textbooks, the state had come to provide absolutely all the needs of the spirit for all the people. Most of the people cooperated in that senseless, ill-advised war and, trapped in the tragedy, paid dearly for it. I think it is fair to say that the latter was in large part the result of the former. Be that as it may, for nearly a century decisions of educational content had been the state's to make, and textbooks either were written by the Ministry of Education or had to meet the criteria of the Ministry. For several years after the inauguration of the school system in 1872, there was freedom to publish and freedom to choose textbooks. But the people who had experienced that period had all died off, so it was only natural that people had come to accept without question that the government determined the content of education, that before publication textbooks at least should be screened by the Ministry of Education. What from my point of view were "national superstitions" came to circulate almost without question. But the Constitution of Japan guaranteed without reservation the freedoms of the mind: thought, conscience, religious belief, expression. If you really thought about it, was it likely that this constitution would permit the state to control the content of education, that domain most crucial to the mind? Education influences the formation of character, so state control of education means that on the issue of what kind of person to become, the people are under the compulsion of the state. To be sure, the phrase *freedom of education* appears nowhere in the constitution. But when you think of all the stipulations concerning freedom of the mind in the constitution, it is not likely that the constitution would permit the state to control educational content, which is at the very foundation of the world of the mind.

I was one of those spineless characters who during the war had taken no action in opposition to the war, had watched powerless from the sidelines as my country met destruction, and could only stand by as many of my generation went to their deaths. The fact that any opposition I might have attempted would have had no effect at all was irrelevant; the experience had left me with spiritual scars. I did not want to let the deaths of several million countrymen be in vain. The rejection of war and the protection of the fundamental human rights that the Constitution of Japan established—weren't they an inestimable heritage bought with the noble blood of my countrymen? The Constitution of Japan was not merely the pride of the Japanese people; it held epoch-making significance in human history. The people should protect those basic ideals of the constitution at all costs and, each according to his own strength, give their all to oppose attempts to destroy these ideals or render them hollow. And isn't it the responsibility in particular of my generation, which survived that tragic war, to see that the people do so? The Constitution of Japan was in force, yet textbooks true to its spirit were blocked from publication, and to swallow one's bile was to allow the destruction of the constitution or its hollowing out. Leave victory or defeat out of account—by fighting all the way in the courts and appealing broadly to the public outside the courts, I would sound the tocsin for the destruction of "national superstitions." If I could only get the people to understand how frightening it is when the state controls the content of education, how horrendous the result when the people give the state carte blanche, victory or defeat in the courts would not matter. This was the fundamental motive that led me to embark on the suit.

In addition, a number of factors—my intellectual path until then, my experience, my character—made it almost inevitable that I would seek to do battle in the courts. First, up until then organizations of researchers, textbook authors, workers in textbook publishing, and the like had mounted repeated movements against the advancement of national thought control via textbook

---

[T]he ultimate goal of these suits is to have the courts declare that the realm of the mind is sacred ground that does not allow the intrusion of the state and to guarantee freedom of thought as a fundamental human right; it is not to argue in court the rights and wrongs of specific historical consciousness and ask the court to decide between arguments. By laying bare in court, in concrete detail, the reality of textbook certification, we are asking the courts to recognize that textbook certification is an illegal intrusion into freedom of scholarship and education, and in that cause many historians and educators have taken the witness stand.

Their testimony aims at making the courts understand that certification, under the pretense of deciding the educational merit of specific examples, is in fact the attempt to force into the textbooks the historical view that the authorities favor and to expunge from the textbooks the history the authorities don't like.

—1981

Source: Ienaga, in Tōyama Shigeki, Kyōkasho kentei no shisō to rekishi kyōiku: rekishigakusha wa shōgensuru (Tokyo: Ayumi shuppan, 1983), pp. 6–7.

certification, and all nine historical associations had petitioned the Minister of Education on this point. But if a movement of opposition to the administrative authorities and appeal of their actions could be mounted at the popular level, then that might do the trick. In the Diet, members of the opposition parties had pursued the issue of textbook approval and cited actual examples, but the authorities had adroitly evaded the issue with "bureaucratic explanations." In the Diet the time allotted the opposition parties for statements was limited, so they could not pursue the same problem forever. The courts, too, were one facet of state power, and there was no guarantee that they would always be fair. But to the extent at least of the constitutional provision of judicial independence and the principle of the law of suits that sets the state and individuals on the same level, it was possible to pull the state down to a position in which it had to respond to charges on precisely our level. According to the rules of open confrontation, the arguments of both parties would be transmitted to society at large and could engage public interest and criticism. Such an arena of battle was available, but it was useless if we did not use it.

Second, for someone like me who was not good at "movements," the courts were the ideal means to advance the struggle. I was not "apolitical," but I knew well that I was a very unpolitical person in the sense of being most maladroit at "politics" and "movements," where a high degree of skill in bargaining and cooperation is very important. To be sure, suits also are part of "politics" in the broad sense, so they require the arts of courtroom tactics, and in constitutional suits emphasizing the arousing of public opinion outside the courtroom over victory in the court, a "movement" is crucial. But suits seemed more appropriate for me: to pour energy first and foremost into deploying in court principles of law and telling evidence, overwhelming the legal arguments and evidence put forward by the other side. Moreover, as a youth I had discovered in *Sollen* a higher meaning than *Sein* and through all the twists and turns of my intellectual development had clung to that conviction, and a struggle that put the emphasis on legality over the rights and wrongs of policy, on finding a clear decision, black or white—in short, a legal battle—seemed to suit my temperament. That thought led naturally to the novel idea of a suit over the constitutionality of textbook certification.

> [M]y interest in the textbook issue goes back to involvement with the lawsuits . . . in my graduate student days at Tokyo University of Education [in the 1980s]. Plaintiff Ienaga Saburō was there, but I wasn't lured into the suits by Ienaga himself. He distinguished scrupulously between his official work, including university instruction, and his own lawsuits. I remember he never missed a single class on account of the suits.
>
> For ten years after I graduated and began teaching at Tokyo Gakugei University, the better half of my life was the lawsuits. I poured my time into the suits. . . . And I learned a great deal. The suits were a comprehensive university—history, education, law. The foundations of my current scholarship lie there.
>
> —A scholar of the younger generation, 1996
>
> Source: Kimijima Kazuhiko, *Kyōkasho no shisō: Nihon to Kankoku no kingendaishi* (Tokyo: Suzusawa, 1996), p. 327.

I had other motives, too; but by disputing textbook certification in court on the basis that it violated the constitution, I confirmed my determination to be a conscientious researcher and educator. Contrary to the fears I had had ahead of time, when the suit was reported in the press, letters of encouragement and support from people I didn't know piled up on my desk. I did not ask for financial support, yet contributions came pouring in. These were entirely unselfish voices of sympathy and valuable contributions of money, and I was moved. Soon a nationwide support group was set up, and it expanded into an organization offering both moral and material support for suits that was long-lasting and involved a large legal team. I could never have paid for the suits out of my own pocket. When the examination of witnesses began, first-class people from all the related areas—beginning with Nambara Shigeru, former president of Tokyo University[1]— willingly became witnesses and gave high-quality testimony that moved those who heard it. They came from the worlds of legal scholarship, education, historical scholarship, teaching, and textbook publishing.

At the time of the previous certification, I had been asked to revise a quarter of my manuscript, including three aspects and six

---

1. Nambara Shigeru (1889–1974): political scientist.

> [The Nanjing Incident Study Group] got its start when our newsletter ran the dialogue between Ienaga and Honda Katsuichi. At that time there was mention of the suits, and people said, "Let's get a study group together," and Fujiwara and the others got together and formed a study group on Nanjing. The connection with the textbook suit was the genesis, the study group came into existence, and thereafter research made very great strides; I think this was one of the very major accomplishments of the textbook suits. And then "Unit 731" was very similar: the dialogue between Morimura and Ienaga ran in our newsletter, and that led to Morimura's joining.* . . . "Nanjing," "Unit 731"—as a result of the textbook suits, research made very great strides.
> —Younger colleague, 1998
>
> Source: Kimijima Kazuhiko, in Rekishi no hōtei, p. 206.
>
> *Honda Katsuichi (1933–): journalist, China reporter. Fujiwara Akira (1922–): historian. Morimura Seiichi (1933–): writer, author of book on Unit 731.

passages that against my will I had either to revise or to delete. Now in 1967 I restored all three aspects and six passages to their original form, but not one of them was approved. Because the deadline for lodging administrative suits had already passed, the suit we lodged first was a suit seeking damages from the state for illegal acts—the rejection in 1963 and the request for changes in 1964; but now we quickly lodged a suit to nullify the rejection of 1967. The former we call Suit #1, the latter, Suit #2; but the trial of Suit #2 went forward and neared its conclusion more quickly. As the likelihood increased that Suit #2 would end quickly in victory for the plaintiff, those supporting the Ministry of Education began to exert themselves to drag out the suit. They had gangs of thugs send threatening telegrams and letters to my house, and to frighten me away from attending court they had a dozen or so men advance on my house in the middle of the night and raise a ruckus by breaking soda bottles. Inside and outside the courtroom, too, the disciples of violence time and again made threats and distributed handbills slandering the plaintiff and the judges. Unable to compete with the elevated arguments and evidence of the plaintiff, right-wing groups supporting the Ministry had no choice but to resort to these sordid means. That the Ministry opposed us with the support of such gangs of thugs speaks volumes about the essence of the suit.

Nor was that all. The Ministry tried in court, openly, to deceive the court with lies. As I mentioned earlier, it was reported orally to us as a reason for rejection that the pictures in the section on the Pacific War were "on the whole too grim." That was manifest fact: it had happened in front of me and several employees of the publisher. Yet in court they told this bald-faced lie: "We said only that the last photograph, entitled 'Ravages of war,' showing a disabled veteran, a photograph cut off at the upper lip and showing an artificial arm, was very grim; it was not a suitable photo for inclusion in a textbook. We did not say, as the plaintiff alleges, that these five photos taken together were too grim." The defense also produced a number of witnesses to give testimony in opposition, but their testimony was crude and didn't stand comparison with that of the plaintiff's witnesses. Moreover, cross-examination generally demolished its worth as evidence.

July 17, 1970, was the day of first judgment for Suit #2. Sugimoto Ryōkichi, chief judge of Petty Bench II (for civil law) of Tokyo District Court, ordered the noncertification voided and then read out the gist of the reasons for the judgment: noncertification in this instance constituted state interference in educational content and violated Article 21, Clause 2, of the constitution and Article 10 of the Fundamental Law of Education. A crowd of several hundred supporters filled the street in front of the court and looked up at the windows, intensely anxious about the judgment to be handed down. When they saw those in attendance flash the V sign from the windows on the second floor, they gave an unpremeditated shout of victory that resounded even inside the court.

The reasons for the judgment were stated in detail: based on the "right to receive an education" in Article 26 of the constitution, "freedom of education" was a constitutional right; the state had no authority over education, but according to Article 23, freedom of education existed in order to allow primary, junior high, and high school teachers to conduct true education; authors of textbooks had the liberty to publish textbooks. Despite the fact that a wave of reactionary jurisprudence had already begun to engulf the courts, the court did not sidestep judgment of the constitutional issues, dealt head-on with the thorny legal issues of "state and education," and handed down its conclusion that text-

Photo 10.1   Ienaga speaking to supporters, September 24, 1969.
Photo courtesy of Ienaga Saburō.

book approval was unconstitutional. As I have noted, the courts had already handed down many judgments declaring that under Article 10 of the Fundamental Law of Education administrative interference in educational content was illegal; but for the first time the Sugimoto judgment raised the issue to the constitutional level. It is no exaggeration to say that this was indeed an epoch-making judgment in the history of the Japanese judiciary. It is attributable to the conscientiousness of Presiding Judge Sugimoto and sitting judges Nakadaira Kenkichi and Iwai Shun, who upheld the independence of the judiciary, but it would not do to overlook the all-out efforts of the plaintiff's counsel, witnesses, and supporters, which made it fundamentally possible for the court to hand down the correct judgment. To be frank, I had not expected right off the bat to win a victory like this, in which the court accepted virtually all of our arguments. Far from it. But that very fact made me feel acutely all over again that when you confront an illegal state of affairs and there is room to fight not with physical force but through appeal to reason, you should not hesitate to assert the truth even if it involves risk.

The textbook suit had primed the pump for a complete reexamination of Articles 21, 23, 26, and other articles of the constitution as they had existed to that time in constitutional scholarship, and new theories had begun to appear in rapid succession. With the appearance of the Sugimoto judgment, that trend moved forward rapidly. After the Sugimoto judgment, books concerning constitutional scholarship could not avoid dealing with the argument that state interference in educational content is unconstitutional. Not only that, but most first-class constitutional scholars came to support—in its essentials if not in its details—the argument of the Sugimoto judgment that the constitution basically protects the freedom of education. One might term it a shift of the terms of debate in the world of constitutional scholarship.

Victory or defeat was secondary. The reason I dared to lodge these suits was that I thought the courtroom was the most effective forum for demonstrating to the people that this strict state control was being carried out through certification. A second reason was that I thought the suits would make most people realize that the state must not encroach on the world of the mind. The Sugimoto decision—that alone is adequate reward.

I've carried on, thanks to all the support, but the time remaining to me has grown short. More than anything, I hope that the younger generation will take up the cause. That younger generation, unfortunately, has lost interest in social and political issues, but I'd really like to see it bestir itself.

—1994

Source: Ienaga, *Ienaga Saburō taidanshū*, pp. 180–181. His interlocutor is Takeda Kiyoko.

Thereafter, however, the storm of reactionary jurisprudence that engulfed the courts gradually became more severe, and the intentions of people with ties to the Supreme Court to apply the brakes to lower-court judgments of unconstitutionality occasionally manifested themselves in crude form. The judges in Suit #1 changed repeatedly, and the hearings were drawn out; finally, on July 16, 1974, judgment was handed down. It had been nine years since we filed the suit. The judgment of Petty Bench III (civil law; presiding judge: Takatsu Tamaki) of the same Tokyo District Court as Petty Bench II was a mediocre one, wholly unable to stand comparison with the excellent Sugimoto judgment, even though that judgment stood as precedent. The conclusion that textbook certification was constitutional and legal was absolutely unacceptable. But, even more troublesome, the legal reasoning that led to that conclusion was inconsistent, and its recognition of facts was a joke. Most astonishing, it took the reasons for noncertification and the requests for amendment and dealt with them not one by one or all together, but by arbitrarily picking some and handing down individual decisions on the rights or wrongs of those. It was as if the court possessed powers of discrimination in matters of history and history education that were a cut above those of the plaintiff or the Ministry of Education. It found the opinions in several of those particulars to be inappropriate and illegal, and to that limited degree it found there was reason for the plaintiff's claims and ordered the state as accused to pay 100,000 yen [about $300 at the 1974 exchange rate] in consolation money. Having argued that it was impermissible for the state to interfere in textbook content, we could not accept the fact that the court ruled on which of the Ministry's opinions and which of the textbook's contents were proper and which were not. Still, even a court so wedded to state power had to concede that the Ministry of Education had been too harsh in its certification. As reactionary as it was, the Takatsu judgment was not a total defeat for the plaintiffs.

In Suit #2 the Ministry had suffered complete defeat. The hearing of its appeal began before Petty Bench I (civil law) of Tokyo Superior Court. From our analysis of its earlier decisions, we knew that the Tokyo Superior Court leaned most strongly in the direction of the authority of the state, and so it did. As if his mind were made up even without a trial, the first presiding judge,

Toyomizu Michisuke, let his prejudices show from time to time—during arguments in court he displayed shameful conduct, dozing and snoring—and was replaced. In the midst of the procedures that must take place when a judge is replaced, the next presiding judge, Azegami Eiji, suddenly brought the trial to an end, and on December 20, 1975, over the protests of the parties, he handed down judgment. Shelving the issue of the constitutionality of textbook approval—that is, not declaring it either constitutional or unconstitutional—he recognized that even in the framework of the existing system, the denial of certification was willful and illegal in not following the current criteria for certification, so he threw out the appeal and handed the Ministry a defeat. It was an inferior judgment, saying that the original judgment had ruled on constitutional issues where there was no need to, but it did not touch on the correctness of the Sugimoto judgment's finding of unconstitutionality, so it did not overturn the constitutional argument of the Sugimoto judgment. On Suit #2, speaking only of results, it was the second consecutive defeat for the Ministry. The three judgments so far—Sugimoto, Takatsu, Azegami—differed greatly among themselves, but in three tries the Ministry of Education had not been able to win even one clear victory. Even under reactionary jurisprudence, the Ministry could not gain the complete legitimation of textbook certification: that fact speaks eloquently of the outrageous nature of the Ministry's conduct.

In Suit #1, the defense appealed the Takatsu judgment, and the hearing is now taking place before Petty Bench V (civil law) of Tokyo Superior Court. In Suit #2, the Ministry filed a final appeal of the Azegami judgment, and it was heard before Petty Bench I of the Supreme Court. One cannot foresee what course the two suits will take from here on, but there are clearly few grounds for optimism. Still, as I have said repeatedly, victory is not the primary point. Immediately after the Takatsu judgment was handed down, I recited a poem to a meeting of my supporters:

Kachimake wa	Win or lose—
sa mo araba are	what matter?
tamashii no	we fight
jiyu o motome	for
ware wa tatakau	freedom of spirit.

Photo 10.2   The scene outside court on the day the Sugimoto judgment was handed down, July 17, 1970. Banner reads: "Plaintiff's Victory." Photo courtesy of Ienaga Saburō.

That has been my consistent attitude toward these suits. From here on out, to be worthy of the support of my many fervent supporters, I'll fight with all my strength.

No matter what happens from now on in the textbook suits, we won the historic Sugimoto judgment and were sustained by the warm encouragement of many supporters, and I always felt good as I headed for court. Even though I was the object of intimidation by gangs of thugs, even though I encountered unhappy decisions like the Takatsu judgment, I did not waver because it was clear that I had the backing of a broad range of people from the worlds of scholarship, education, and public opinion, and because I had unwavering confidence less in the verdict of the courts than in the verdict of history. A second poem I read to the group immediately after the Takatsu judgment expresses this confidence:

Akanesasu	The ruddy sun
hi wa kageredomo	may be obscured,
'Iyahate no sabaki'	but as I await
o tanomu	"Judgment Day,"
kokoro kumorazu	my spirit is unclouded.

In comparison to the textbook suits, I had no stomach at all for the issue of the move to Tsukuba, which developed at my university after I had filed the textbook suits. In the summer of 1964 President Miwa Tomoo put out a tale of wanting to move to Tsukuba Research Park City [a new development about an hour east of Tokyo] because a broad tract of land was available there, while the existing campus of Tokyo University of Education was small. Thus began the issue of the move to Tsukuba. Favoring the move were President Miwa and the faculty councils of Sciences and Physical Education; the Faculty of Letters, of which I was a member, was overwhelmingly opposed. We were opposed because for research and education in the humanities and social sciences it was best to stay in Tokyo, the city that is the center of academic and artistic activity and the locus of many research collections, and a move to Tsukuba would entail a major step backward. Over a long period, university bodies all discussed the pros and cons of

---

The judgment of Petit Banc #3 of the Supreme Court that brought the suits to a close did not declare unconstitutional the intrusion of the government into the content of education, and that had been the ultimate goal of the suits; rather, it judged, in the light of scholarly opinion at the time of the certification, whether there were mistakes that were difficult to overlook in the opinions of the certifiers. Hence for me it is not something with which I can be satisfied fully.

—1998

Source: Ienaga, Foreword, in *Rekishi no hōtei*, p. 3.

moving, but they reached no agreement. Finally on June 10, 1967, over the opposition of the Faculty of Letters, the university council forced through a resolution in favor of securing the land for the move to Tsukuba. The faculty council of the Faculty of Letters recalled Dean Ōshima Kiyoshi and the other two representatives who had given tacit approval to this forced vote and declared it would not cooperate in the move. Thus began a sharp antagonism between the faculty council of the Faculty of Letters, on the one hand, and, on the other, the faculty councils of the four faculties—education, sciences, agriculture, and physical education—where majorities favored the move, and the optical research center, all of them led by President Miwa. Nearly all the students opposed the move to Tsukuba; excepting only physical education, the student governments of the four faculties launched a struggle against the move to Tsukuba. The next year, in June 1968, the student government association of the Faculty of Letters, in which those favoring the move controlled the executive, carried out a lock-out of the campus—in other words, a Paris Strike—and we faculty could not get to our offices. Then this student sect that favored the move joined with similar student sects from other faculties to form an all-university struggle committee and carry out a lock-out/occupation of buildings on the main campus.

Just about this time, disturbances arose one after the other all across Japan at public and private universities, beginning with Tokyo University. In the case of the other universities, they took the form for the most part of conflicts between students and administrators, but the case of Tokyo University of Education was unique in that it was a confrontation between the Faculty of Letters, on the one hand, and, on the other, the president and the five faculty councils that supported him. Because the Tokyo University of Education "disturbance" had its origin in the exceedingly mundane argument over which was better, the present site or Tsukuba, people at large were forever seeing it as simply an "internal dispute." Not only did the faculty council of the Faculty of Letters have to carry on the fight alone and unassisted, but on the axiom that faculty were all pawns of the power structure, the students of the Paris-Strike sect also mounted a violent assault on the main faction of the faculty council of the Faculty of Letters. Thus, the faculty in the majority in the faculty council came under assault pincer-like, fore and aft.

[T]he intensification of textbook certification and the planning for Tsu-kuba University, while differing in that the one was about pre-college edu-cation and the other about college education—were both the fruit of the Ministry of Education's policy aimed at advancing government control of education and therein have the same root. In that sense the struggle against textbook certification and the struggle against plans for Tsukuba University were basically actions arising from the same spirit, not the chance coincidence of unrelated events (they were different in that in one I acted as a single citizen, in the other as a professor, but they were alike in the broad sense that I acted as educator), and both I took as tasks I could not not take on. . . .

The Tsukuba opposition and the textbook lawsuits seemed like a dou-ble burden on me, but the prosecution of the lawsuits rescued me from frustration with the Tsukuba issue.

—1978

Source: Ienaga, *Tōkyō Kyōiku Daigaku Bungakubu—Kōei to junan no sanjūnen* (Tokuma, 1978), pp. 243–244.

But in fact the true aim of those favoring the move to Tsu-kuba was not the size of the campus; this became plain finally after they made clear what they called their "new vision of the university." Their aim was to build a "new university," embody-ing in letter-perfect form the law of university management that the Ministry of Education and the financial circles had long envis-aged. The goals were as follows: to make the production of human talent its main goal, responding in this way to the desires of the financial world; to focus authority in the hands of the president and vice president; to abolish faculty councils and bring to an end the running of the university through the collective will of the faculty; to set up in their place an organ whereby outsiders could take part in running the university, thus allowing the interference of the financial world and others; to control student life strictly; and so on. After the Tsukuba issue arose and throughout the process of the "dispute," these aims could be seen all the more clearly in that they appeared in the administrative policies pur-sued by the successive presidents, the Science Faculty Council, and others of the pro-Tsukuba faction supporting them. Ever since the establishment of faculty councils, the faculty council of the Faculty of Letters had urged the democratization of the university, and it had cooperated in the university council's decision of June 21, 1962, under President Tomonaga's leadership establishing democratic rules (later called the "Tomonaga principles") for running the university. I described those events at the beginning of chapter 9. The university council's procedures themselves were something the faculty council of the Faculty of Letters could not accept. Contrary to the "Tomonaga principles," the university council did not work to reconcile the president's forceful advocacy of the move and the various faculties, and it ignored the opinion of the Faculty of Letters. This was all the more true because the real aim of the "move" forced through in this fashion was not a larger campus but the creation of an antidemocratic "new university." So the chasm that opened up between the faculty council of the Faculty of Letters, on the one hand, and the president and the other faculties, on the other, became unbridgeable.

In the faculty council of the Faculty of Letters, a minority favored the move, and in the other faculties minorities opposed the move, so if one took into account all the members of all the faculty councils, opinion was probably 60:40 in favor of the move. What is more, practically all the students opposed the move to Tsukuba. Yet the pro-move faction disregarded this large opposition and pushed forward by all means the majority decision of the university council. Considering that the goal was not only a move to a different prefecture but also fundamental changes in the running of the university, one has to say that those favoring the move did not work toward a full reconciliation of opinions within the university. The faculty council of the Faculty of Letters sharply disavowed the use of force that the occupation of the school buildings by the students represented. But since, of course, the root cause was the forced advocacy of the move by the authorities, the council argued that the solution to the "dispute" lay in getting the agreement of as many faculty members of the whole university as possible; to respond to violence with violence and to think only of suppressing the students was not an attitude educators should take. The faculty council of the Faculty of Letters itself, even while under attack from the rear by some students, held firmly to a policy of debating with any and all groups that asked, so long as they were students, and not refusing to meet with students even if the result was kangaroo-court impeachment of the faculty.

Not even the university council could disregard opinion within the university. At the end of 1968 it decided to convene a one-time all-university meeting, but it was blocked by the hawkish faction centered in the Faculty of Science, and the meeting did not take place. On February 28, 1969, on his own and without consulting any university organ, the acting president, Miyajima Tatsuoki, brought in the riot squad and ended the occupation. At the same time, he instituted a lock-out and placed the campus under the complete and sole control of the president. That brought the normal functioning of the university to a complete halt, so it fully deserves to be called a coup d'état. Under this authoritarian control, the freedom of thought and expression of faculty and students was taken away, and on occasion, the authority that by law belonged rightfully to the faculty council of the Faculty of Letters was infringed. In September of that year, when the faculty council of the Faculty of Letters sought to resume business, the president used the riot squad to remove students who had entered the campus peacefully, and we saw a state never seen before—the "crushing of instruction" by the president. In order to avoid shutting down the faculty—the worst possible situation for the students, even worse than repeating the year, the faculty council of the Faculty of Letters swallowed its shame and resumed instruction. But in April of the next year, 1970, the univer-

---

Today the world is going through drastic upheaval—the collapse of the Soviet Union, for example. I was born in 1913, but I never dreamed that the Soviet Union would not last as long as my own life.

I think the key to the Soviet Union's collapse lies in the fact that the one-party dictatorship of the Communist Party suppressed freedom. In Japan anti-Soviet fever is strong, and there are a good many politicians who speak ill of the Soviet Union; but the same people who are inciting anti-Soviet fever are aping the Soviet Union in the field of education—exercising control of education.

—*Interview, 1992*

Source: Ienaga, *Taidanshū*, pp. 130–131. His interlocutor is Osanai Mieko.

sity council decided on a code of standards for faculty appointments and framed the conditions so that those who opposed the university council's decision to move to Tsukuba could not be appointed or promoted. This brought personnel matters of the faculty council of the Faculty of Letters to a halt. In September of the same year, at a meeting at which the representatives of the Faculty of Letters were not present, the university council resolved that responsibility for the "unrest" lay wholly and unilaterally with the Faculty of Letters and even went so far in its recklessness as to call for the resignation of three professors: Hoshino Shinichi, former dean of the Faculty of Letters; Irie Yukio, another former dean; and Ienaga Saburō.

Up until that point, other universities and scholarly associations and society at large had watched the dispute at Tokyo University of Education from the sidelines, regarding it as an "internal dispute." Now they finally came to realize how large the problem was. Against behavior that ignored the regulations of university administration—laying the responsibility that belonged with the whole university solely on the Faculty of Letters and, without listening to the suggestions of that faculty council, passing a motion demanding the resignation of professors—the Association of Japanese Scholars, the society of legal scholars, the faculty councils and societies of many universities, and various other groups and individuals flooded the university council with expressions of protest. It was apparently the initial intent, should the faculty council of the Faculty of Letters not bring about the resignations, that the university council should force them through, but in the glare of public criticism, the university council was unable finally to do so. The faculty council of the Faculty of Letters resolutely refused the demand of the university council and protected the jobs of the three professors. The pressure of public opinion blocked the illegal firing of professors before the fact—a rare occurrence.

In that same year of 1973, the Diet forced through the Tsukuba University law, and, in accordance with the earlier vision, Tsukuba University opened, a very antidemocratic university utterly unlike the existing national universities. Miwa Tomoo, former president of Tokyo University of Education and the man who instigated the move to Tsukuba, was appointed first president. When the proposed Tsukuba University law had been submitted to the Diet, universities, scholarly associations, and the general public came to recognize for the first time that the dispute over the move to Tsukuba by Tokyo University of Education was not simply an issue internal to one university but had enormous significance that shook the very roots of university self-government. Resolutions in opposition from 57 universities—2 university councils and 111 faculties—and declarations of opposition by about 8,000 academics were made public, and a movement developed inside and outside the Diet to stop the enactment of the law. But by this stage, it was too late.

Having opposed Tsukuba University from first to last, the faculty council of the Faculty of Letters finally had broken out of its isolation and now enjoyed broad support from outside the university, but the draft law became law, and the law was revised; so Tokyo University of Education would close its doors at the end of March 1978, and the Faculty of Letters would cut its faculty and students to zero by the end of March 1977. Each year after 1973 the numbers of faculty and students decreased, and in the academic year 1976–1977 the only students left were seniors. With only an occasional person to be seen, the Ōtsuka campus came to have a deserted feeling about it. It called to mind a graveyard. Some students who stayed back a year were at the university until March 1978, so the few faculty necessary to their education stayed on. But the faculty council met for the final time on March 30, 1977, and then the members scattered. For many years the faculty council of the Faculty of Letters had been in the vanguard of university democratization, but now the council was a thing of the past. Still, it merits special mention that the majority did not fall apart, and it maintained its solidarity to the last; minor differences of opinion were ironed out, and the common interest prevailed. This held true even after the forced decision to relocate and in particular even after the Miyajima "coup d'etat," even in the face of repeated and indescribable persecution, and after a boycott of the faculty council in the first half of 1969 by the minority that favored the move to Tsukuba. In most cases, when organizations are driven into extremely unfavorable situations, defectors and splinter groups appear, and the group falls apart. After the boycott group left, a few of them rejoined the faculty council, but there were virtually no defections from the faculty council.

By coincidence, March 1977—the month the Faculty of Let-

> These fifty years [since the war] have been a time of upheaval after up-
> heaval. In my case, it has been one stunning change after another: as
> a child: Taishō democracy; as soon as I matured, fascism, war, postwar
> democracy, then the reverse course [of the Occupation], and a time of
> material plenty and spiritual poverty.
>
> —1994
>
> Source: Ienaga, Taidanshū, p. 168. His interlocutor is Takeda Kiyoko.

ters was reduced to zero—happened also to be the date of my retirement, and on April 1 I retired from Tokyo University of Education. I had begun teaching at Tokyo Higher Normal School in
1944, and I had become a full professor in the Faculty of Letters
in 1949, Tokyo University of Education's first year as a new university. So I had taught at the Ōtsuka campus for thirty-three
years, twenty-eight of these at the new university. I had spent the
greater part of the most important period of my life at this campus, and the period, from the first day of the new university's Faculty of Letters to its very last, was at the same time the major part
of my career. So my retirement was different from ordinary retire-
ments, and I was unable to suppress deep emotion.

I was fortunate in being able to carry out my research in so
favored an environment. And even if it was not always the best
use of my talents, and even though people around me advised me
to stop getting so involved and devote myself only to my own research, I threw all my scant energy into the cause of the democratic operation of the university via the faculty council of the
Faculty of Letters. In the era of President Tomonaga, we had advanced to stand at the fore of democratization among the national
universities, but with the appointment of President Miwa Tomoo
and the issue of the move to Tsukuba, Tokyo University of Education went straight downhill. In the end, Tokyo University of Education was demolished and replaced with the antidemocratic university called Tsukuba University. The faculty council of the
Faculty of Letters had carried on the fight, alone and unassisted,
since the beginning of the dispute. I was one of its members, and
in comparison with my colleagues I had done nothing at all. But
for me, sickly all my life and getting on in years, it had been con-

tinuous suffering that was difficult to endure: rancorous debate at faculty council meetings that lasted for long hours and sometimes late into the night; "mass negotiation" with students, bathed in violent boos and hisses; and the rest. Earlier, university professors were envied for having the best of all jobs—short working hours and the freedom to study whatever they wanted. But in time of trouble there was no job worse than being a university professor. I keenly lamented that fact. Be that as it may, the faculty council of the Faculty of Letters defended the self-government of the university and its democratic management tenaciously, and bearing up under illegal persecution, it kept the faith to the end. When I look back at its indomitable spirit, I cannot help feeling satisfaction in my heart of hearts that from first to last I was a member. The democratization of the university that the Faculty of Letters had pursued consistently ever since its founding was destroyed for the sake of Tsukuba, but the outstanding individuals nurtured in the nearly thirty years of the Faculty of the new university are even now active in the front ranks of society, and the seeds the Faculty sowed will surely lead to a bountiful harvest for Japan. As for the heroic efforts of the faculty council of the Faculty of Letters to protect university self-government, the day will surely come when those efforts receive high praise in the history of Japan's universities.

I said that in the textbook suits, victory in court alone was not primary. In the same sense, if you restrict your gaze to the short run, the fight of the Faculty of Letters of Tokyo University of Education ended, of course, in defeat, but if you look at it in the broader view, I firmly believe that it was not in vain. I have not the slightest regret that, weak though I was, I devoted a good deal of effort to the struggle for right of the Faculty of Letters of

---

Come to think of it, while these lawsuits were in progress, we relied on Ienaga for moral strength. From now on we have to figure out a new arrangement, how to do battle with these forces [behind the attacks on textbooks].

—*Younger colleague, 1998*

Source: Kitajima Manji, "Zadankai," in *Rekishi no hōtei*, p. 217.

Tokyo University of Education. Not only that, but I can look back with satisfaction that I had a truly meaningful university career. At first glance, the textbook suits and the struggle at Tokyo University of Education seem utterly unrelated, but in fact that is not the case. The "strengthening" of certification and the concept of Tsukuba University have a common essence: both stem from the same root—namely, reactionary educational policy. The man who was chair of the "defense group" for the Ministry of Education in the textbook suits led the drive to move to Tsukuba and became Tsukuba University's first president: that fact alone is symbolic testimony to the fact that the two are virtually identical twins.

I was a lover of books with the modest ambition of leaving a single volume of academic research to the world when I died. Yet to my great surprise, the textbook suits and the fight to democratize Tokyo University of Education became my life's work. In each case I did little more than let myself be pulled along by the great abilities of many kindred souls, but I count it the glory of my life that I took part in activities "to defend intellectual freedom" that without doubt will live through all history. Not much time is left me, but I pray earnestly that I will hold to my convictions until my dying day.

INDEX

academic achievement tests,
172–74
aggression, 167
Amaterasu, Ōmikami, *35,* 44–45
Arai Akira, 175
Asai Jihei, 58
atrocities, *138. See also* Unit 731
August 15, 1945, 124
autobiography in Japan, 20–21
Axis, 23
Azegami Eiji, 185

Bellah, Robert N., 4–5
Bible, 35, 95. *See also* Christianity
Buddhism, 2, *57,* 90, 92, 94–95,
101. *See also* Shinran; Shōtoku
Taishi

censorship, x, 86–87, *105, 109,*
126–27
China, 1, 7, 86, *116, 138, 167;*
China war, 36, *89,* 100, 101–2,
111; Eighth Route Army, 7. *See
also* Manchurian Incident
Christianity, 5, 34, 92. *See also*
Bible; Uchimura Kanzō
code of ethics for teachers, 159,
169
communism, ix, 125, 134, 163
Communist Party, 140
Constitution of Japan (1946), 13,

17, 127, 137–38, 139–41, 152,
158; Article 9 of, *152;* Articles 21
and 23 of, 181, 183; Article 26
of, *153,* 181, 183; and democracy, 19, *105,* 151; and fundamental human rights, 139, 149,
163, 176–77; and peace, 42,
151; popular awareness of, *164,*
168; revision of, 151–52; and
textbook certification, 179. *See
also* Meiji Constitution
courts, 16, 162–68. *See also* Ienaga
Saburō; Supreme Court; Tokyo
District Court; Tokyo Superior
Court

Dalton Plan, 42
Diet, 159, 178, 193

Edo era, 2, 8
education laws, 137, 156
education, role of, 8–9, 42, *47, 53,*
63, 70–71, 109, *121;*
education trials, 169–73
emperor [Hirohito], 88, 124
emperor system, 66, 67, 149
England, 7, 50, *89,* 100, 111
Europe, 24

F., Professor, 32
family system, *117, 155*

197

February 26 Incident [1936], 88
fifteen-year war, 2, 6–9; See also
Pacific War; World War II
First Tokyo Municipal Middle
School, 49–54, 57, 62–64, 68
Fujiwara Akira, 180
Fukuhara Rintarō, 144–46, 152
Fukuyama Toshio, 97
Fukuzawa Yukichi, 33
Fundamental Law of Education,
137, 158, 160; Article 10 of, 77,
173, 174, 181–82
Futamata Incident, 168

Germany, 47, 136; Nazi Germany,
7, 23, 147, 149
Great Depression, 32

Hamaguchi Cabinet, 35
Hanzōmon, 26, 49
Hayama, 54
Hiraizumi Kiyoshi, 81–83, 88–89,
104, 105
Hirata Atsutane, 82
Hirata Toshiharu, 83–84
Hiroshima, 10, 157, 160
Hirotsu Kazuo, 168
historical materialism. See
Marxism
Historical Materials of Japan, 99, 100
Historiographical Institute, 82,
98–101, 104, 105, 106, 112
Honda Katsuichi, 180
Hoshino Shinichi, 192
Hozumi Yatsuka, 24, 87

Ienaga Chiyo (mother), 27–31, 54,
64, 123
Ienaga Miyako (wife), 20, 116, 142
Ienaga, Saburō: court testimony
of, 6, 13, 14, 57, 131, 171; and
democracy, 7–8, 11–13, 19–20,
47, 105, 127, 128, 134; health of,

and career, 2, 18, 55–56, 100,
101, 102, 113, 194–95; health
of, during war, 115–16, 123;
health of, in youth, 55, 113;
helplessness of, to stop war: 6,
12, 53; Ienaga on, 23, 76–77,
105, 177, 183; impact of, 14–15,
134; and Japanism, 47, 67, 70–
71, 75, 89, 92, 95–96, 112, 117;
judgments in, 10–11; lawsuits
brought by, 7, 16, 71, 93, 175–
87, 195, 196. See also courts;
Marxism; poetry by Ienaga Saburō; support movement for Ienaga's lawsuits; textbook certification
Ienaga Saburō, books by: Chronology of Paintings in the Yamato
Style, 3, 5, 101; Criticism of the
Courts, 3, 169; Development of the
Logic of Negation in Japanese Intellectual History, 3, 4, 6, 63, 95,
118; A Historical Examination of
the Independence of the Judiciary,
3, 169; History of Early Painting in
the Yamato Style, 3, 101; History of
University Self-Rule, 3, 5, 154; Japan's Past, Japan's Future: Odyssey
of a Historian, 6, 16–17, 20, 21,
23; A New History of Japan, 20,
154; On the Assimilation of Foreign
Culture into Japan, 3, 101; The Pacific War, 5, 6–8; The Progress of
the Country, 129–32, 135; Studies
in the Kingship of Shōtoku Taishi,
3, 97, 101; Studies in Medieval
Buddhist History, 3, 101; Works of
Ienaga Saburō, x, 4
Ienaga Saburō's brothers and sisters, 28, 30, 31, 40, 54, 66
Ienaga Shintarō (father), 7, 27–37,
39, 123
Ihara Saikaku, 125

Ikeda [Hayato] Cabinet, 153
Ikezaki Tadataka, 36, 111
Imanaga Hiroaki, 175
Imperial Academy, 113, 115, 118
Inoue Kiyoshi, 114
Inoue Mitsusada, 114, 135
intimidation, 180, 186
Irie Yukio, 192
Ishikawa Tatsuzō, 103
Italy, 23, 37
Iwai Shun, 182

Japanese Communist Party, 140
Japanism: Ienaga Saburō and, 47, 67, 70–71, 75, 89, 92, 95–96, 112, 117; Ienaga Shintarō and, 34, 37

Kaizuka, 27
Kamata, *26*, 115, 116
Kamo Mabuchi, 118
Kanda Takahira, 33
Kant, Immanuel, 19, 23, 75
Karasawa Tomitarō, 40, 43, 45–46
Karatsu, 39–40
Katō Hiroyuki, 33
Katō Kanji, 35
Kawai Incident, 43–44
Kenseikai, 35. *See also* Minseitō
Kimijima Kazuhiko, 16
Kishi [Nobusuke] Cabinet, 152
Kitabatake Chikafusa, 82, 89
kokoro, 18
Konishi Shirō, 135
Korea, 7, 46, *136*
Korean War, 134
Kōsaka Masaaki, 120–21
Kumagai Hiromu, 169
Kumamoto, *25*
Kuno Osamu, 120
Kuroha Kiyotaka, 17–21
Kuroita Katsumi, 81–83
Kusunoki Masashige, 82

Kusunoki Masatsura, 64
Kyoto, 89

Liberal-Democratic Party, 9
London Conference, 35

Maizuru Incident, 166
Manchurian Incident, 69, 72, 87, 102, *105*, 111, 133
Maruyama Masao, 23, 121
Marxism, 5, 69, 71–74, 92, 117, 127–28, 140, 149
Masaki Hiroshi, 4, 22, 123, 168
Matsukawa Incident, 168
Mazaki [Jinzaburō], 88
Meiji Constitution, 13, 44, 105, 127, 138, 163, 164. *See also* Constitution of Japan
Meiji emperor, 41, 46, 87
Meiji era, 34, 47, 112
Meiji Restoration, 46, *113*
militarists, 35, 133, 141. *See also* Japanism
military, 7, 27, 28–30, 102–3, *125*, 138, 148
mimponshugi, 33–34
Minear, Richard H., and *Victors' Justice*, ix–x, 7
Ministry of Education: and academic protests, 135–36, 177–78; in court judgments, 23, 173, 174, 184; and Ienaga's lawsuits, 1, 7, 9, 20; and Ienaga's texts, *78*, 157–62, *167*, 181; and *The Progress of the Country*, 130, 154; and supporters, 180–81; and textbook certification, 41, 155, 176; and Tokyo University of education, 143, 189. *See also* textbook certification
Minobe Tatsukichi, 34, 84–85; at Imperial Academy, 113–15; in Ienaga's writing, 4, 18–19, 34,

75, 76, 85–86; influence of, on
Ienaga, 66–67, 70, 90, 121, 163
Minseitō, 37. *See also* Kenseikai
minshushugi [democracy], 34n2
Minshūtō, 156
Mishima Yukio, 24
Mito Studies, 89
Miwa Tomoo, 187, 188, 192, 194
Miyajima Tatsuoki, 13, 191, 193
Miyazawa Toshiyoshi, 151
Mizuno Hironori, 36, 111
Morimura Seiichi, *151*
Mori Ōgai, 43–44, 92–93
Moritani Kimitoshi, 16
Motoori Norinaga, 118
moving pictures, 3, 126
mythical origins of Japan, *35,*
44–45

Nagoya, 2, *25,* 28
Nakadaira Kenkichi, 182
Nakagawa Kazuo, 115, 116
Nakamura Kōya, 82
Nambara Shigeru, 179
Nanjing, Rape of, *89, 180*
Nara, 89–90
Narita airport, *93*
Narita Senri, 50–52, 57, 62
national polity, 41, 86, 87–88. *See
also* Amaterasu; Japanism
Natsume Sōseki, 58
neo-Kantianism, 73–78, 94, 95,
178
Nichiren, 86
Niigata, *25,* 105–6, 112
Niigata Higher School, 3, 101, 103,
105–8, *109, 110,* 113, 118
Niimura Yoshihiro, 140–41
Ninomiya Sontoku, 40–41
Nishida Kitarō, 119
Nishimura Shinji, 46, 58, 65, 66,
70
Nishioka Toranosuke, 99, 104, 135

Occupation of Japan: early re-
forms, 124–25, 127, 133, 136,
141, 154; and reverse course,
134, 139, 147, 154, 166, *194;*
U.S. control of, *134*
Oda Nobunaga, 65
Okano Tarō, 40, 42, 92
Okinawa, *25, 136*
orthodoxy. *See* Japanism. Osaka,
25, 27, 30, 40
Ōshima Kiyoshi, 188
Ōtsuka, *26,* 115, 142. *See also* Tokyo
University of Education
Ōuchi Hyōe, 151
Oyama Hiroshi, 163, 172, 175
Oyama Uhachirō, 43

Pacific War, 28, 36, 108–9, 115,
120–21, 128, *134,* 175; and Ienaga's powerlessness, 6, 13,
128; in Ienaga's writing, ix–x, 5,
6–7, 8, 16, *89, 132, 148,* 155,
159, *161;* and prewar education,
8–9, 136, 175. *See also* August
15, 1945; World War II
Pal, Radhabinod, ix–x
Peace Preservation Laws, 13, 37,
125, 139, 163
Pearl Harbor, 89, 108
peasant uprisings, 155
people's rights movement, 34, *113,*
125
poetry by Ienaga Saburō, 59–62,
185, 187
pollution, *93*
Popolo Case, 164, 168
Portugal, *138*
positivism, *73,* 97–98, 128, 130,
131
press code, 127

rearmament of Japan, 147, 151
reverse course. *See* Occupation of
Japan

Rickert, Heinrich, 74, 75
Russia. *See* Soviet Union
Russo-Japanese War, 2

S. (colleague), 111
Sachiura Incident, 168
Sakai Toshihiko, 35
Sakamoto Tarō, 97, 111
Satō Eisaku, 9
Satō Shinichi, 135
Security Treaty, 152
Sein/Sollen. See neo-Kantianism
Seiyūkai, 35
Sendai, 116, 123
sexual practices, Japanese and
    American, *145*
Shibanuma Choku, 143, 146, 147
Shibata Kiyo, 39
Shigakkai, 82–3
Shiga Yoshio, 123
Shimazaki Tōson, 58, 62, 73
Shimbō Iwatsugu, 65–66
Shinran, 4, 5, 19, 94, 95
Shiromuro Masujirō, 87
shoshin, 17, 18, 20, 22
Shōtoku Taishi, 4, 5, 19, *57,* 90
Shōwa terror, 69
shutaisei. See subjectivity
Sino-Japanese War, 36
Smedley, Agnes, 89
Smithsonian Institution, 10
Snow, Edgar, 89
socialism, 70, 77, 125
Soviet Union, 7, 8, *125, 191*
subjectivity *(shutaisei),* 19
Suetsumuhana, 125–26
Sugimoto Ryōkichi, 181, 182, 183,
    186
Sugo Incident, 168
support movement for Ienaga's
    lawsuits, *12,* 14–16, 179
Supreme Court, *10–11,* 14, 22–23,
    168, 184, 185, *187,* 194

Taishō democracy, 40, 42, 44, 47,
    69, 89, *194*
Taishō emperor, 46–47
Takami Jun, 139–40
Takatsu Tamaki, 184, 185, 186–87
Takayama Iwao, 118, 120
Takeoka Katsuya, 115
Takigawa Incident, 84
Tale of Genji, 86
Tamenaga Shunsui, 125
Tanabe Hajime, 73, 75, 117,
    118–21
Tanaka Kōtarō, 169
Tanizaki Junichiro, 23–4
Taoka Reiun, 4
teachers' unions, 169, 172–74
"Tenchan," 88
textbook certification, 15, 76–77,
    136, 154–59, 171, 175; and Jap-
    anese Constitution, 13, 14, 169,
    177, 178, 179; Ienaga's experi-
    ence of, *167,* 171; and Ministry
    control, *71,* 177–78, *189. See also*
    Ministry of Education
textbooks, 2, 9, 22, *73, 85, 155,* 177,
    179
Tokuda Kyūichi, 123
Tokugawa era. *See* Edo era
Tokugawa Ieyasu, 65
Tokutomi Sohō, 36, 65
Tokyo District Court, 166, 169,
    172, 175, 181
Tokyo Higher Normal School, 3,
    115, 142, 143, 194. *See also*
    Tokyo University of Education
Tokyo Higher School, 68, 69, 81
Tokyo Humanities and Science
    University, 142–44
Tokyo Imperial University, 21, 66,
    78–79, 81–84, 102, *105;* Faculty
    of Letters of, 78–79, 97–99. *See
    also* Tokyo University
Tokyo Superior Court, *12,* 184, 185

Tokyo University, 145, 164, 188
Tokyo University of Education: as
    Ienaga's place of employment,
    3, *105, 179;* faculty activism at,
    135, 137; move to Tsukuba of,
    1, 11, 13, 16, 187–88; political
    struggles at, 142–47, 152–54,
    194–95. *See also* Tokyo Higher
    Normal School
Tomonaga Shinichirō, 153, 190,
    194
Tōyama Shigeki, 135
Toyomizu Michisuke, 185
Toyotomi Hideyoshi, 41, 65
Tsuda Shinichirō, 33
Tsuda Sōkichi, 66, 97, 130
Tsuji Zennosuke, 81–83, 97, 98,
    104, 113
Tsukuba Research City, 1, 11,
    187–94
Tsukuba University, *189,* 193
Tsukuba University law, 192
Tsurumi Shunsuke, 120

Uchimura Kanzō, 4, 5, 19, 162
Ueki Emori, 4
Uemura Seiji, 111–12
Uesugi Shinkichi, 24, 87
Unit 731, 89, 148, *180*
United States, x, 3, 21, 24, *145;*
    and the Pacific War, 36, *89,* 100,
    106, 108, 109–10; and postwar

control of Japan, 6, 19, 134, 139,
    147, 152. *See also* Occupation of
    Japan
university self-government, 165
university unrest, *93,* 188
Ushigome, *26,* 40, 43, 54

Vietnam, American war in, ix, *136*

Wagatsuma Sakae, 145, 151
war crimes trials, ix–x, 133
war guilt, *132*
Watsuji Tetsurō, 90, 119
Wells, H. G., 65
Windelband, Wilhelm, 74, 75
women, role of, 20, *117, 121, 143,
    155,* 157
World War I, 28
World War II, 8, 23, *78, 125. See also*
    Pacific War

Yamazaki Ansai, 82
Yanagita Kunio, 111, 112
Yanaihara Tadao, 22, *123,* 145
Yashiro Yukio, 100
Yasuda Hiroshi, 15
Yatsushiro, 28, 30
Yochō-machi Primary School, *26,*
    40, 49, 54
Yokokawa Toshio, 140–41
Yoshida, 33

Zeami, 17

ABOUT THE AUTHOR AND TRANSLATOR

ABOUT THE AUTHOR

Ienaga Saburō (1913–) is one of the most distinguished Japanese historians of the twentieth century. Beginning his academic career during Japan's fifteen-year war, he wrote and edited literally hundreds of books. They deal with Japanese intellectual, social, cultural, and art history, and range in time from the sixth century A.D. to the Pacific War. With the public at large, he is most famous for his suit against the Ministry of Education. This thirty-two-year attempt (1965–1997) to have the Ministry's "certification" of textbooks declared unconstitutional ended in defeat, but the effort will surely go down in history as one of the academic and political landmarks of postwar Japan.

ABOUT THE TRANSLATOR

Richard H. Minear is an intellectual historian of Japan and translator of many volumes of prose and poetry that relate to the Pacific War and Hiroshima. His most recent book is *Dr. Seuss Goes to War* (1999). He teaches at the University of Massachusetts in Amherst.